DRUGS, SEX, AND INTEGRITY

What Does Judaism Say?

DANIEL F. POLISH
DANIEL B. SYME
BERNARD M. ZLOTOWITZ

Illustrated by José Diaz

UAHC Press · New York · New York

Library of Congress Cataloging-in-Publication Data

Polish, Daniel F.
  Drugs, sex, and integrity : what does Judaism say? / Daniel F.
Polish, Daniel B. Syme, Bernard M. Zlotowitz ; illustrated by José
Diaz.
      p.   cm.
  Includes bibliographical references.
  Summary: Uses a case study format to explain Jewish law as
expressed in the Bible, the Talmud, and the Jewish Reform movement.
  ISBN 0–8074–0459–4 : $10.00
  1. Ethics, Jewish—Juvenile literature. 2. Jewish law—Reform
Judaism—Juvenile literature. 3. Judaism and social problems—
Juvenile literature. 4. Drug abuse—Religious aspects—Judaism—
Juvenile literature. 5. Sex—Religious aspects—Judaism—Juvenile
literature. [1. Jewish law—Reform Judaism. 2. Ethics, Jewish.]
  I. Syme, Daniel B. II. Zlotowitz, Bernard M. III. Diaz, José (Diaz-
Portalatin), ill. IV. Title.
BJ1285.P65   1991
296.3′85—dc20   √ 90–28763
                                                        CIP
                                                        AC

This Book Is Printed on Recycled Paper

To my mother, Sonia Syme
The finest teacher of responsa with whom I have
ever studied, and whose thousands of students,
young and old, rise up and call her blessed

Daniel B. Syme

With love—
To my children and their spouses:
Debbie and Rick (Greenberg), Robin,
Richard and Joni (Cohen), and Alice.
And to my grandchildren, Marissa and Andrea

Bernard M. Zlotowitz

In loving gratitude for the legacy left by my
grandfather, A. H. Friedland—who was also
published by the UAHC

Daniel F. Polish

ACKNOWLEDGMENTS

This book has benefited from the careful and constructive input of many friends. Dr. Zena Sulkes, Robert Tornberg, Sonia Syme, Rabbis Walter Jacob, Martin S. Rozenberg, Selig Salkowitz, Leslie Gutterman, Paul Yedwab, Gary Bretton-Granatoor, Emily Feigenson, and Howard Laibson read one or more manuscript drafts and offered numerous helpful comments.

We offer special thanks to Aron Hirt-Manheimer, UAHC editor of *Reform Judaism,* for his sensitive and brilliant editing, to Stuart L. Benick, UAHC Director of Publications, for his usual masterly transformation of our raw manuscript into a finished volume, and to Annette Abramson and Dorian Kreindler for copyediting the text with such a keen eye.

We extend our gratitude to Eppie Begleiter, Marian Brewer, Ruth Melchet, Thelma Cohen, Fern Prag-Browne, Ruth Hayes-Barba, and Vivian Mendeles, who typed parts of the manuscript in its various stages.

Finally, we mention with blessing the name of Rabbi Solomon B. Freehof ז״ל, who during his life encouraged us to pursue this project, and whose memory remains an inspiration to the Jewish world as a whole.

CONTENTS

INTRODUCTION

As you begin to read this book, you probably will be encountering the world of Jewish law for the first time.

The lack of emphasis on Jewish law, or *halachah*, among liberal Jews stems from Reform's initial focus on prophetic values rather than Torah legislation. We are enriched as Jews, however, when we know what Jewish tradition says about how we should conduct our lives in virtually every situation.

Jewish law has driven and shaped Judaism in the past and continues to do so today. *Halachah* is dynamic, as responsive to the human condition today as it was in eras past.

We hope this book will be your point of entry into the world of Judaism's greatest rabbis and scholars, who have guided the Jewish people since the time of Moses.

Here you will meet new teachers who will help you confront human dilemmas we all face.

CHAPTER
1

THE PATH OF JEWISH LAW

Halachah can be likened to the legal system in the United States, where the original source of authority was the Constitution with its Bill of Rights, which established privileges and responsibilities for every American citizen.

In the more than two centuries of America's existence, however, countless situations have arisen that were not anticipated by the Constitution or by its Bill of Rights. Therefore a process was required to interpret and expand the law in the situations not specifically covered. When a legal dispute arose, the question was placed before a judge, who listened to the arguments on both sides and then issued a decision. If one of the parties to the argument felt that the judge had not ruled appropriately, he or she had the right to appeal the decision to a higher court—up to the United States Supreme Court.

Once the Supreme Court agreed to consider the case, its judgment became the definitive law of the land. Often the decision and the arguments of the justices, including both minority and majority opinions, were issued in writing. That decision became a *precedent*, an extension of American law that served as a guide in future legal cases.

This growing body of law eliminated the need for many similar cases to come to trial. From time to time the Supreme Court struck down or modified laws in response to social and political change, such as the ending of segregation in schools, guaranteeing voting privileges for all Americans, and granting women the right to an abortion. These and other rulings demonstrated that the high court could enact major revisions so long as the rulings did not violate the letter and spirit of the United States Constitution and its Bill of Rights.

Jewish responsa literature, collections of rabbinic answers to Jewish legal questions, constitutes a similar body of legal decisions. In Jewish law, however, the Torah is the fundamental document, and rabbis serve as the judges. Orthodox Jews regard the Torah as God-given and therefore eternally true and unchangeable.

Jewish tradition, however, recognizes *two* Torahs: one given by God at Mount Sinai and written down by Moses, the "Written Torah"; and one conveyed orally to Moses at Sinai, the "Oral Torah." The Oral Torah is understood to have been passed down by word of mouth from generation to generation until about 200 C.E. when it was committed to writing as a collection of laws called the *Mishnah*. In time, the

Mishnah itself required interpretation, resulting in the *Gemara*. Together the *Mishnah* and *Gemara* comprise the Talmud, the greatest legal text of Judaism. According to Jewish tradition, the Written Torah and the Oral Torah are regarded as divine in origin.

In order to apply Torah and talmudic laws to new life situations, a great first-century Jewish scholar, Rabbi Ishmael, introduced a special system for interpreting the Torah and Talmud. His thirteen rules of interpretation became strict guidelines for the application of Jewish law to modern life.

Here is an example of how the Oral Law has shaped the ways Jews practice their Judaism. The Torah tells us simply and directly not to work on Shabbat. Generations of our people have read these words and felt obligated to obey them because God, who created heaven and earth, and delivered us from slavery in Egypt, has "commanded" that we not work on Shabbat. What could be clearer? The Torah, however, does not provide a definition of work. So the *Mishnah* attempted to make the law more specific, listing thirty-nine types of activity characterized as work. The *Gemara* was even more specific, enumerating a whole range of activities included under each of the thirty-nine broader categories.

The Torah also states that we must not light a fire on Shabbat. Jews asked, "What about a fire that had been started before the Shabbat?" The rabbis answered that it is permissible to make use of such a fire. "Can you use a fire that a non-Jew starts on Shabbat?" Again, the answer was yes. More recently people have wondered if they could use electricity on Shabbat, or whether it was also a kind of fire. That question was the subject of a *responsum*—the exchange of a question and answer concerning interpretation of Jewish law. Modern Orthodox rabbinic authorities concluded that electricity was indeed the equivalent of fire and therefore Jews could *not* turn on electric lights or appliances on Shabbat. The responsa literature thus extended the injunctions of Torah and Talmud to apply to circumstances that did not exist when they were written—and could, therefore, not have been anticipated by the rabbis. Such new answers then became precedents for similar questions arising in subsequent years.

Most liberal Jews do not accept the belief that God is the author of the Written Torah or the Oral Torah. They hold that human beings inspired by God wrote both. Liberal Jews, however, study Jewish law and observe many mitzvot as a matter of personal conviction, not because "God said so." This differing perception of the binding nature of *halachah* constitutes a fundamental difference between liberal and Orthodox Judaism.

Whether or not you believe that Torah is divinely given, the responsa process illustrates how Jewish law and Jewish values have been and continue to be applied to life circumstances that are relevant to you. Rabbinical answers issued centuries ago continue to speak to us today. The moral and ethical teachings of Judaism, whether God-given or of human origin, offer us a way to respond as Jews to tough modern dilemmas as we approach the twenty-first century.

Before we begin, however, we want to introduce you to some great Jewish scholars, spanning a period of years almost fifteen times longer than the history of the United States! Here are just a few of the most important "judges" of the Jewish people.

AUTHOR/EDITOR	TEXT/COLLECTION	DATE	COUNTRY	CONTENTS
God, according to the Orthodox. Human Beings, who were divinely inspired, according to liberal Jews.	Torah (Five Books of Moses)	c. 1200 B.C.E	Sinai Desert and Land of Israel	History and laws of the Jewish people.
Human Beings	Prophets and Writings	400 B.C.E.–200 C.E.	Land of Israel	History, laws, prayers, and prophetic values. The Torah, Prophets, and Writings constitute the Hebrew Bible, known as *Tanach*.
Rabbi Judah the Prince	*Mishnah*	200 C.E.	Land of Israel	Laws, ethics, and customs of Jews.
Rabbi Jonah and Rabbi Jose	Palestinian Talmud (also known as the Jerusalem Talmud)	Fifth century C.E.	Land of Israel	Legal commentary on the *Mishnah* with scatterings throughout of ethical teachings, parables, and history.
Rav Ashi and Rabbi Rabina II	Babylonian Talmud	Sixth century C.E.	Babylonia	Legal commentary on the *Mishnah* with scatterings throughout of ethical teachings, parables, and history.
Amram Gaon	*Siddur Rav Amram* (Prayer book)	853–856	Spain	Arranged complete order of prayers for use of Jewish community in Spain.
Rabbenu Gershom ben Judah (known as "Light of the Exile")	His responsa are cited throughout rabbinic literature, especially in the works of Rabbi Meir of Rothenburg	960–1040	Germany	All aspects of Jewish law.
RASHI (acronym for Rabbi Shlomo ben Yitzchak)	Of his responsa, 360 are preserved in *Sefer Hapardes* (Book of the Garden) *Teshuvot Rashi* (Responsa of Rashi) and other books	1040–1105	France	All aspects of Jewish law.
Rabbenu Tam (Rabbi Jacob ben Meir)	*Sefer Hayashar* (Book of the Upright—published in Vienna in 1811)	1100–1171	France	Lenient interpretations of law when stringent rulings would cause great financial hardship.

AUTHOR/EDITOR	TEXT/COLLECTION	DATE	COUNTRY	CONTENTS
MAIMONIDES (Rambam—acronym for Rabbi Moses ben Maimon)	*Mishneh Torah* (Second Torah) and *Yad Hachazakah* (The Mighty Hand)—a fourteen-volume collection	1135–1204	Spain and Egypt	All aspects of Jewish law.
NACHMANIDES (Ramban—acronym for Rabbi Moses ben Nachman)	*She'elot u-Teshuvot* (Responsa—originally published in Venice in 1523)	1194–1270	Spain	All aspects of Jewish law.
Ba'al Haturim (Rabbi Jacob ben Asher)	*Arba'ah Turim* (Four Rows—first published in 1475) Divided into four parts: 1. *Orach Chayyim* (Path of Life) 2. *Yoreh Deah* (Teacher of Knowledge) 3. *Even Ha'ezer* (The Stone of Help) 4. *Choshen Mishpat* (The Breastplate of Judgment)	1275–1340	Spain	All aspects of Jewish law.
Joseph Karo	*Shulchan Aruch* (Set Table—originally published in 1567)	1488–1575	Land of Israel	Covers the whole of Jewish law; has the same divisions as *Arba'ah Turim*.
Rama (Rabbi Moses Isserles)	*Mappah* (Tablecloth) for Joseph Karo's *Shulchan Aruch*	1530–1572	Poland	Added the traditions of Eastern and Western European practices to Karo's Sephardic practices.
Chofetz Chaim (Rabbi Israel Meir Hacohen Kagan)	*Mishnah Berurah* (Clear Study) Six volumes	1838–1933	Poland	Practical everyday Jewish law and observance.
Rabbi Moshe Feinstein	*Igrot Moshe* (Letters of Moses) Eight volumes	1895–1986	United States	Covers virtually every aspect of Jewish law.
Rabbi Solomon Freehof	*Reform Jewish Practice Reform Responsa Recent Reform Responsa Current Reform Responsa Contemporary Reform Responsa New Reform Responsa Today's Reform Responsa*	1892–1990	United States	Jewish law from a liberal perspective.

AUTHOR/EDITOR	TEXT/COLLECTION	DATE	COUNTRY	CONTENTS
Rabbi Isaac Klein	*A Guide to Jewish Religious Practice*	1905–1979	United States	Jewish law from a Conservative perspective.
Rabbi Walter Jacob	*American Reform Responsa Contemporary American Reform Responsa*	1930–	United States	Jewish law from a liberal perspective.

CHAPTER

2

ALCOHOLISM AND DRUG ABUSE:
Does Judaism Sanction Getting High?

In 1986 a seventeen-year-old teenager, whom we shall call David R., was stopped for speeding on a Midwest interstate highway. The police officer smelled alcohol on David's breath and gave him a Breathalyzer test, which determined that he was legally intoxicated. David was arrested for drunk driving.

At a preliminary hearing, David's attorney asked the judge to be lenient, considering that David had no previous record. The court transcript notes that the judge asked David how his parents felt about his actions. David replied that his mother and father were very angry but added that as a Jewish family they often drank as part of Jewish ritual: wine on Shabbat each week, four cups of wine at the Passover seder, even hard liquor in the synagogue on Purim.

"I know what I did was wrong, Your Honor," said David, "but I started drinking in observance of my religion."

Shocked, the judge, who was not Jewish, adjourned the hearing and announced that he wished to study the matter further.

Was David correct? Does Jewish tradition encourage consumption of alcohol. What do Jewish texts say?

THE CRISIS OF TEENAGE ALCOHOLISM AND DRUG DEPENDENCE

There are few problems of greater concern today than the epidemic of adolescent alcohol and drug abuse. The number of teens with serious addictions entering alcohol and drug treatment centers has swelled to record levels in the last decade. Teenage deaths attributable to alcohol and drug abuse run into the thousands every year.

The "why" of alcohol and drug abuse remains a mystery. A release from tension, a cheap "high," a pleasurable feeling, a new experience, peer pressure—these are some of the reasons offered by young people who subsequently became "hooked." Casual "recreational" or "social" indulgence often leads to addiction and consequently poses a threat to life. Alcoholism and drug abuse are self-inflicted diseases. Recovering alcoholics and drug addicts warn that the best course is to steer entirely clear of these substances.

ALCOHOLISM: A JEWISH RESPONSE IN THE BIBLE

Alcoholism is as old as the Bible and always was regarded as contrary to Jewish teachings. Care of the body was enjoined by God: "For your own sake, therefore, be most careful. . . ." (Deut. 4:15) Though this verse actually refers to a prohibition against making idols, the rabbis expanded it to include the general health and welfare of a person.

Drunkenness Can Lead to Tragedy

The Bible points out the perils of excessive consumption of wine and strong drink: loss of judgment, loss of wisdom, loss of control over one's behavior, and other dire consequences. Noah and Lot stand out as examples of the close association between drinking and forbidden sexual conduct. Noah drank wine, became intoxicated, and lay uncovered within his tent. He was, in this way, degraded in the eyes of his sons.

Later in the Bible we read that Lot's daughters made him drunk, then seduced their father: After Lot fled from Sodom and Gomorrah in response to God's command, his daughters feared they might never marry and have children, so:

> That night they made their father drink wine, and the older one went in and lay with her father; he did not know when she lay down or when she rose. The next day the older one said to the younger, "See, I lay with Father last night; let us make him drink wine tonight also, and you go and lie with him, that we may maintain life through our father." That night also they made their father drink wine, and the younger one went and lay with him; he did not know when she lay down or when she rose.
>
> Thus the two daughters of Lot came to be with child by their father. The older one bore a son and named him Moab; he is the father

of the Moabites of today. And the younger also bore a son, and she called him Ben-ammi; he is the father of the Ammonites of today.

> (Genesis 19:33–38)

The Moabites and the Ammonites became two of the greatest enemies of the Jewish people. This story, then, ties drunkenness to incest and to strife. Both stories reflect an underlying attitude of concern about the potential effect of alcohol on people's judgment and values.

The Prayer of a Drunkard Is Ignored by God

God is portrayed in Jewish literature as criticizing the drunkard. In fact, the Talmud explicitly states that those who drink to excess are not permitted to pray.

Drinking of Wine Can Lead to Perversion of Justice

Out of concern that too much wine will destroy his ability to judge, the mother of King Lemuel (Solomon) commands him not to drink:

> Wine is not for kings, O Lemuel;
> Not for kings to drink,
> Nor any strong drink for princes,
> Lest they drink and forget what has been ordained,
> And infringe on the rights of the poor.
> (Proverbs 31:4,5)

The Hebrew prophets were outspoken in their denunciation of those who abused alcohol. Isaiah castigates "the drunkards of Ephraim . . . who are overcome by wine" (28:1), and drunkenness in general:

> They are confused by wine,
> . . . dazed by liquor;
> . . . muddled in their visions,
> They stumble in judgment.
>
> (28:7)

Ezekiel predicts that Jerusalem, degraded by drunkenness, will be conquered:

You shall drink of your sister's cup,
So deep and wide;
It shall cause derision and scorn,
It holds so much.
You shall be filled with drunkenness and woe.
The cup of desolation and horror,
The cup of your sister Samaria—
You shall drink it and drain it,
And gnaw its shards;
And you shall tear your breasts.

(23:32–34)

To the prophet Hosea, indulgence in wine destroys reason:

. . . wine destroy[s] the mind of My
people . . .

(4:11–12)

The Psalmist taught that a drunkard is unworthy of respect:

They reeled and staggered like a drunken man,
all their skill to no avail.

(107:27)

Speaking from experience, the author of Proverbs warned of the perils of guzzling wine and strong drink:

Wine is a scoffer, strong drink a roisterer;
He who is muddled by them will not grow wise.

(20:1)

Do not be of those who guzzle wine,
Or glut themselves on meat;
For guzzlers and gluttons will be impoverished,
And drowsing will clothe you in tatters.

(23:20–21)

In the end, it bites like a snake;
It spits like a basilisk.
Your eyes will see strange sights;
Your heart will speak distorted things.

(23:32–33)

ALCOHOLISM IN RABBINIC LITERATURE

The rabbis never outlawed alcohol and hard drink, recognizing their ritual value when used in moderation. At the same time, they spoke directly about the evils inherent in overindulgence, condemning drunkenness as sinful. Aaron's sons, Nadav and Avihu, "offered before the Lord alien fire, which He had not enjoined upon them" (Lev. 10:1), and "they died." (Lev. 10:2) Immediately following this episode God "says" that they (Aaron and his sons) may not drink "wine or other intoxicant." (Lev. 10:9) The Midrash assumes that this juxtaposition indicates that "the two sons of Aaron died only because they entered the sanctuary drunk."

Maimonides states:

Just as it is prohibited for a priest to enter the sanctuary because of intoxication, so it is prohibited for anyone, priest or layman, to offer normative instruction when drunk . . . unless he is instructing on a point we can assume is obvious to everyone already.

Interpreting Leviticus 10:11, Maimonides concluded that intoxicated priests were not permitted to teach.

One Midrash Compares Drunkenness to Different Types of Animal Behavior

Now Samael, the fallen angel, had come to Noah that morning and asked: "What are you doing?" He answered: "I am planting vines." "And what are they?" "The fruit is sweet, whether eaten fresh or dry, and yields wine to gladden man's heart." Samael cried: "Come, let us share this vineyard; but do not trespass on my half, lest I harm you."

When Noah agreed, Samael killed a lamb and buried it under a vine; then did the same to a lion, a pig, and an ape, so that his vines drank the blood of all four beasts. Hence, though a man be less courageous than a lamb before he tastes wine, yet after drinking a little he will boast himself strong as a lion; and, drinking to excess, will become like a pig and soil his garments; and, drinking yet more, will become like an ape, lurch about foolishly, lose his wits and blaspheme God. So it was with Noah.

(Robert Graves and Raphael Patai, *Hebrew Myths, The Book of Genesis*, p. 120)

The Rabbis Taught That Drunkenness Is Responsible for Crime

When a person has had too much to drink, all self-control and awareness are lost (Talmud and Maimonides), and the ultimate consequence is that the individual is estranged from both God and humanity. (Talmud)

According to some rabbinic authorities, drunkenness was the cause of exile for Judah and Benjamin (Midrash), and drunkenness led to the downfall of Adam. Rabbi Meir said, "The tree of which Adam ate was a grapevine, for nothing brings as much woe over man as wine." (Talmud)

Being of Clear Mind Was Not Only Necessary for Priests But Also for Judges

When ruling on a capital case, a judge was prohibited from drinking wine the entire day. (Talmud) Just as crucial was the other side of the coin: Jewish law held a defendant responsible for misdeeds and crimes, even though they may have been committed in an intoxicated state. (Talmud)

The Rabbis Were More Critical of Women Drunkards Than of Men Who Drank to Excess

This is no surprise, since nearly all literature, be it rabbinic or secular, Jewish or non-Jewish, throughout the ages, was male-oriented. Hannah prayed with such fervor that Eli, the priest in charge of the Tabernacle at Shiloh, mistakenly assumed she was drunk and scolded her: "How long will you make a drunken spectacle of yourself?" (I Sam. 1:14)

The Apocrypha, a collection of books from the biblical period that were not included in the Bible, vilified drunken wives: "A drunken wife will goad anyone to fury. She makes no effort to hide her degradation." The Talmud goes even further in its condemnation of drunken women and describes how debased they can become: "One glass is good for a woman; two are a disgrace; with three she opens her mouth [in lewdness]; with four she solicits in complete abandon even an ass on the street." (Talmud)

A MORE TOLERANT VIEW OF ALCOHOL IN RELIGIOUS SETTINGS

Though the rabbis displayed disgust with alcoholism in general, they were by no means opposed to the consumption of wine in moderation, both for religious and therapeutic purposes.

The rabbis acknowledged that drinking wine in moderation (no more than ten cups) was helpful in alleviating certain emotional symptoms, such as prolonged depression while mourning the death of a loved one. They also recommended wine as a treatment for mild depression, quoting Psalms 104:15: "wine gladdens the human heart." (Talmud)

Above all, wine was required by Jewish law for certain ritual purposes, though on occasion substitutes were permitted. It is a mitzvah to drink wine for *Kiddush*. Raphael Patai has written that the special blessing for wine raises it above the level of ordinary drink, which in a way is "performing a small act of communion with the Creator."

The Talmud interprets the biblical commandment "Remember the Sabbath day to hallow it" (Exod. 20:8) to mean: "Remember it over wine at its beginning." And in the time of the Temple, the drinking of wine or "strong drink" was part of certain holiday rituals. (Deut. 14: 25–26)

The Talmud not only allowed but encouraged drunkenness under certain religiously controlled conditions. In a departure from the strict behavioral demands of the other days of the year, on Purim it was a mitzvah for an adult to get drunk. In fact, you were required to get so drunk that you couldn't tell the difference between "Cursed be Haman" and "Blessed be Mordecai." There were attempts to moderate this injunction, reducing drunkenness on

Purim. Total abstention on Purim, however, was regarded as a sin.

Thus, Jewish tradition teaches that wine could bring joy and happiness and that moderate consumption of wine could help people overcome fear and buoy up the spirit.

DRUG DEPENDENCE: A JEWISH RESPONSE

While the rabbis have much to say about alcoholism, they did not impose specific laws against substance abuse, which suggests that this was not a problem in the talmudic era. The few isolated references are cautionary: Rav said to Chiyya his son, "Do not take drugs" (Talmud); that is, even as a medicine because they are habit-forming. According to the Rashbam, "Your heart will draw you to them and you will come to lose a great deal of money." Even for a cure, then, you should not take medication provided there is some other way to be healed. Today, of course, we follow the instructions of our family physicians with respect to medication.

Modern Jewish legal scholars base their ban on drugs on the recognition that they are harmful to the body—for anything that causes harm to the body is antithetical to Judaism. (Talmud and Maimonides)

The Talmud, for example, states that "King Hezekiah hid the book of remedies and the wise men agreed with him." Maimonides reasons that the king did this because the "cures" were foolishness with no curative value. But it is also possible that the king had the book hidden because the drugs mentioned were addictive and therefore potentially harmful to his people.

One can also apply general biblical views on human welfare to the damaging consequences of addictive drugs. While the verse "When you build a new house, you shall make a parapet for your roof, so that you do not bring blood guilt on your house if anyone should fall from it" (Deut. 22:8) referred originally to making a railing on the roof to prevent accidents, the rabbis expanded the injunction to mean one must avoid bringing anything into the home that can cause bodily harm. To do so, according to the rabbis, would be in violation of God's teachings.

The sages of the Talmud also opposed any behavior that fostered uncontrollable lust, for overindulgence (of alcohol or drugs) interferes with the highest values of Judaism—the study of Torah and the performance of mitzvot.

In summary, aside from the use of stimulants on prescribed occasions to fulfill a mitzvah or the use of medication to cure disease, the ingesting, smoking, or sniffing of drugs was and is prohibited as a violation of God's commandments.

YOUR ANSWER

Now that you have studied the traditional Jewish positions on alcohol and drug use, write out what you think the judge should have said to David. Support your answer with Jewish sources.

THE JUDGE'S DECISION

Though David had clearly violated the law in driving while intoxicated, the judge was intrigued by David's assertion that Jewish practice encouraged or tacitly permitted excessive drinking. Therefore, before imposing sentence, the judge consulted with Jewish scholars in the local community.

In a subsequent hearing, the judge told David the following:

1. There is no basis in Judaism for any claim that excessive alcoholic consumption and/or drug use is encouraged.
2. Jewish tradition limits alcoholic consumption to fixed times and settings, and then solely for specific religious or therapeutic purposes.
3. Jewish tradition condemns alcoholism and drug abuse as unhealthy, demeaning, and contrary to Jewish values.

In view of the fact that David had no previous criminal record, the judge decided to be relatively lenient. David's driver's license was suspended for six months, pending his successful completion of a program at a driving school. In addition, David was ordered to perform 150 hours of community service in local charitable institutions.

In imposing the sentence, the judge warned David that any further violations would result in a much harsher penalty. Finally, the judge suggested that David study his Jewish tradition more carefully. Had he done so and taken it seriously, he might not have found himself in this unfortunate situation.

3

PREMARITAL SEX:
Rabbi, May I?

Dear Rabbi:

I am very upset and hope that you can help me. You always taught us that Judaism has much to teach about the real world. Now that I am a freshman in college, I really need advice.

Specifically, I need to know what Judaism says about premarital sex. I have never asked my parents this question, since it would probably embarrass them. In our home sex is not a comfortable subject. Rabbi, can you give me some guidance?

I look forward to hearing from you.

Love,
Cindy

Before reading the rabbi's response, consider the following overview of traditional Jewish attitudes about human sexuality.

No single Jewish view of sex exists. Rather, one could say that our sages have expressed conflicting attitudes—some puritanical, others more permissive. All biblical and rabbinic writers agree, however, that marriage is the proper domain of sexual relations.

IN THE BIBLE

Biblical authors portrayed human sexuality as coming into the world after Adam and Eve de-fied God by eating from the tree of knowledge of good and evil. In most biblical passages sexual intercourse is presented as diminishing one's ritual purity.

For three days prior to receiving the Ten Commandments, for example, Israelite men were commanded: "Approach not unto a woman" (Exod. 19:15), so that they would be holy enough to hear and accept God's words.

Following sexual relations, a couple was required to undergo ritual purification. "And if a man should lie with a woman with seed of copulation, then they shall bathe themselves in water." (Lev. 15:18)

In addition, in order to restrict sexual relations to husband and wife, a long list of taboos and prohibitions regarding illicit sexual relationships were enacted. There were severe punishments for violators. The Bible prohibits adultery (Exod. 20:13) and condemns incest and bestiality (Lev. 20:11ff.) as crimes punishable by death. Such acts were associated with heathen nations: "And you shall not walk in the customs of the nation, which I am casting out before you; for they did all these things, and therefore I abhorred them." (Lev. 20:23) Even King David was reprimanded by the prophet Nathan and

punished by God for his adulterous relationship with Bathsheba and the deliberate murder of her husband, Uriah. (II Sam. 11:1–17; 12:1–23)

IN THE TALMUD

By talmudic times, while the rabbis viewed sex primarily as serving the purposes of procreation, they did not object to lovemaking by husband and wife for sensual pleasure.

Sexual intercourse was encouraged between a husband and wife, especially on Friday night, when it was considered a mitzvah! One of Ezra's ten *takkanot* (regulations) was "that garlic be eaten on Fridays" (Talmud) because garlic was considered an aphrodisiac, heightening one's sexual appetite.

SEX EDUCATION IN THE RABBINIC PERIOD

The mitzvah of "be fruitful and multiply," the rabbis reasoned, was more likely to be fulfilled if people married young and enjoyed sex. It was usually the father who prepared daughters for marriage and counseled them thus: "Act modestly before your husbands: do not eat bread before your husbands, do not eat greens, do not eat dates at night nor drink beer at night. . . ." (Talmud)

Why? Certain foods and drink were to be avoided because they were thought to decrease sexual desire. Eating bread may cause uncomfortable fullness, eating greens may cause mouth odors, and eating dates and drinking beer may result in gas and physical discomfort. The laws of *niddah* (menstrual cycle) probably were taught by the mother.

The Talmud and the Codes deal with *taharat hamishpachah*—"purity of the family"—rules regulating sexual behavior. The *Gemara* states that it is forbidden to engage in sex during menstruation, in daylight, or in a lighted room. R. Hisda ruled that a man is "forbidden to perform his marital duty" in the daytime, since, according

to Abaye, he might observe something repulsive in his wife and therefore consider her disgusting. The great scholar Raba, however, overcame the halachic prohibition of refraining from sex in daytime by simply darkening the room. In fact, the *halachah* states that a scholar may engage in sex with his wife in daytime provided he blocks the sunlight. Here again the rabbis recognized the importance of sex and adjusted the rules to make it possible both day and night.

SEXUAL RIGHTS FOR WOMEN

A Jewish husband was prohibited by biblical law from denying his wife sex: "Her food, her clothing, and her conjugal rights he shall not diminish." (Exod. 21:10) In fact, the Talmud asserted that denying a wife sex constituted cruel and unusual treatment. Therefore, the *Gemara* went so far as to set the minimum number of times a married man was *required* to have sexual intercourse with his wife, taking the husband's occupation into account: for men of financial independence, every day; for laborers, twice a week; for ass-drivers, once a week; for camel drivers, once in thirty days; for sailors, once in six months.

PREMARITAL AND EXTRAMARITAL SEX

Sex prior to marriage or outside of marriage was prohibited by the rabbis, who set up elaborate and rigorous rules and regulations to confine sex to the marital bed. Those caught engaging in sex outside of marriage were punished. Men and women were segregated at weddings, at funerals, and in the synagogue because a woman was thought to be capable of arousing sexual thoughts in men through her appearance, her touch, and even through her voice.

Women, whether single or married, had to be chaperoned at all times, even with relatives. Great care was taken so as to guard a woman's virtue from suspicion. The rabbis generally tried to impose severe restrictions on all physical contact between men and women in public or private. Women, for example, were not supposed to walk in front of men, lest they arouse excitement. Intercourse with surrogates or prostitutes, as well as attendance at sexually oriented shows, was forbidden.

To summarize, while the attitude during the biblical period demonstrates great ambivalence about sex, the talmudic and rabbinic attitude was that sex was a normal, healthy human impulse. That being the case, rules and regulations, some quite strict, were drawn up to regulate sexual behavior so that a husband and wife could live a moral and healthy life.

YOUR ANSWER

Now that you have studied some of the Jewish sources, assume the role of Cindy's rabbi and write an answer to her letter. After you have finished, see what the rabbi wrote.

THE RABBI'S LETTER TO CINDY

Dear Cindy,

Thank you for your very thought-provoking letter. First of all, I want you to know how pleased I am that you feel free to ask me the question you raised. I'm here for you now and in the future.

There is no way in which I can answer your question fully in a letter. Please let me know when you will be in town and we can talk in person. For now, however, let me try to tell you what Judaism says in an abbreviated way.

First of all, sex is not a sin in Judaism. As a matter of fact, God's first commandment in the Torah instructs Adam and Eve to "be fruitful and multiply," make love and have children.

The story is the key to your question, Cindy. In Judaism, sex within the marriage relationship is healthy and encouraged. On the other hand, sex outside of marriage is strongly discouraged.

I know that as a college freshman you will face many new pressures. They may be frightening at times.

The best advice I can give you, then, is to think and trust the values with which you have been raised. Above all, never be embarrassed or reluctant to say no.

I'll look forward to seeing you soon.

Sincerely,
Rabbi

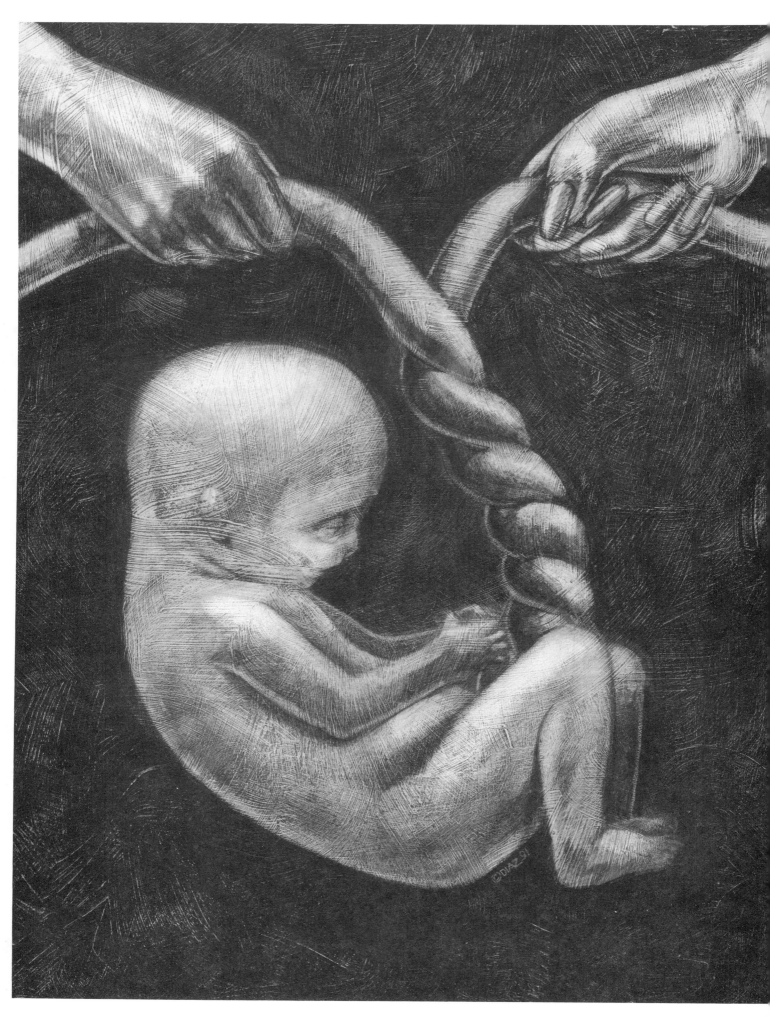

CHAPTER
4

SURROGATE PARENTHOOD:
Whose Baby Is It?

From the moment of her birth she was famous, the subject of a court trial covered extensively in the news media.

"She" was Baby M. Her father, Dr. William Stern, was a child of Holocaust survivors, the last person left to carry the family name. His wife, Elizabeth, suffered from a disorder that made giving birth dangerous to her health. The Sterns, therefore, made an arrangement with another woman, Mary Beth Whitehead, who, through a clinical procedure, would carry Dr. Stern's child in her womb. The terms of the agreement were drawn up in a contract. As agreed, Dr. Stern's sperm was medically implanted in Mrs. Whitehead and a child was conceived. But when the baby was born, Mrs. Whitehead decided that she wanted to keep the child and refused to give it up.

The Sterns took the matter to court, demanding that Mrs. Whitehead fulfill the terms of the contract by giving them the baby.

MICHAEL'S DILEMMA

Michael had a special interest in the Baby M case. He read every article about it and watched the nightly news to catch a glimpse of Baby M and to hear the latest reports about the court battle.

Michael knew that he, too, had been conceived through the process of artificial insemination. So the questions raised in the case of Baby M had a lot to do with how Michael thought about himself and his parents, who were Jewish.

While the trial was in progress, some of his Catholic friends told him that the Catholic Church had issued an "instruction" that rejected all modern technologies that help parents conceive; it rejected "in vitro fertilization" and artificial insemination. The Church also rejected surrogate parentship contracts—the kind that the Sterns and Mrs. Whitehead negotiated. Michael wondered if Jewish tradition would disapprove of how he was conceived. Perhaps he was not even considered truly Jewish. When he asked his parents what Judaism taught, they said: "We never thought about it. We just knew that we wanted you, a baby of our own. We didn't consult with any Jewish authority." But Michael wanted to know. He asked his rabbi: "Am I Jewish? Does Judaism think that I was born in an acceptable way?"

IN THE BIBLE

Judaism understands what it means for an individual to want children but be unable to conceive them. The first mitzvah recorded in the Bible is to "be fruitful and multiply." (Gen. 1:28) Our Torah recounts the sad tales of matriarchs who ached to bear children but could not. In Psalm 113 the image of the once-"barren woman" who now dwells in her house as a "joyful mother of children" represents the clearest expression of how the birth of children can convert feelings of emptiness to fulfillment.

But what does the Torah say about attempts to change that condition? Isaac prays to God on behalf of his barren wife, Rebekah; Rachel also prays; and the matriarchs Sarah, Leah, and Rachel give their handmaids to their husbands as concubines—women who bear children in place of the wife. Hagar, Abram's concubine, however, or Bilhah and Zilpah, the concubines of Jacob, were not surrogate mothers. In their society husbands typically had more than one wife. The concubine, considered the wife's personal property, nevertheless was also a wife—albeit a second-class wife.

Studies of Mesopotamia, the area in which many biblical stories are set, reveal that a woman of higher status, such as Sarah, generally brought to a marriage certain property, including a handmaid whom she could give to her husband. The Bible clearly states that Sarai gave Hagar "to her husband to be his wife." (Gen. 16:3) The child (of Abram and Hagar), however, was to be counted as Sarai's own (Gen. 16:2), while, after the birth, Hagar remained Abram's wife as was the custom. Because of friction with Sarai, though, Hagar had to leave Abram's household, but her departure was not because Hagar simply had been "hired" to bear a child and leave after her job was completed; she was considered part of the family.

This biblical response to childlessness represented the highest "technology" of the ancient period. Today we have at our disposal a variety of advanced techniques: artificial insemination, in vitro fertilization, surrogate motherhood.

Thus, while the Bible offers insight into the pain of childlessness and describes the manner in which a "barren woman" could acquire a child, it does not provide a definitive answer to Michael's questions. Perhaps a review of *halachah* can provide Michael with a more direct response.

The Catholic Church bases its rejection of fertility technology on the idea of "natural law," the teaching that the world is as God wished it to be. Judaism differs, instructing that human actions are essential in completing God's design. Nature alone, for example, does not yield bread or bricks. To bake bread *we* must cut grain and grind flour; to form bricks *we* must mix mud and straw. That is what it means to say people are copartners with God.

The late Professor Seymour Siegel, of the Jewish Theological Seminary, once wrote: "When nature plays a trick on us, we have to outwit it." That kind of "outwitting" also is part of being a partner with God. Perhaps that is one reason why Jews are drawn to careers in medicine.

TOUGH HALACHIC QUESTIONS

In the course of the Baby M case, modern halachic scholars were concerned primarily with questions of personal status: Is the child legitimate? Have the parents committed adultery? What will be the religion of the newborn child?

In Judaism, discussion of this issue begins with recognition of the blessing of parenthood. In the creation story, the phrase "be fruitful and multiply" is repeated to the animals, then commanded of Adam and Eve, and again of Noah at the "new creation" following the Flood. As a result, Judaism has historically encouraged people to become parents, but within certain limits.

The Bible considers adultery a sin. According to Jewish law, a child born of an adulterous relationship (when a married woman has sexual relations with a man other than her husband) is called a *mamzer* (illegitimate). (Deut. 23:3 and

Talmud) However, a child born to unmarried parents is considered legitimate, unlike in American civil law, which deems such a child illegitimate.

Modern technology has complicated these distinctions. Today a man's sperm can be implanted in a woman by means other than through sexual intercourse, specifically through artificial insemination or in vitro fertilization—life created outside of the body in a test tube, using sperm taken from the prospective father and an ovum removed from the prospective mother. The fertilized egg is then implanted in a surrogate mother, who carries the fetus to term and gives birth to a baby.

If the ovum of the prospective mother came from the body of another man's wife or if the host mother was married to a man other than the prospective father, has adultery been committed?

THE DILEMMA OF ARTIFICIAL INSEMINATION

In the case of artificial insemination with donor sperm, is the process adulterous and the offspring illegitimate? Rabbinic authorities are in disagreement. Some rabbinical authorities have declared the process adulterous and the offspring illegitimate. They base their opinion on Lev. 18:20, which prohibits a man from having sexual relations with his neighbor's wife. The text goes on to state: "You shall not give any of your seed . . ." On the basis of this verse, Rabbi J. L. Zirelsohn, author of *Ma'archei Lev*, prohibited artificial insemination of a married woman on the grounds of adultery.

Other rabbis disagree. Ben Zion Uziel, the former chief Sephardic rabbi of Israel and a foremost interpreter of Jewish law, and the late Rabbi Solomon B. Freehof, a leading Reform halachic authority, argue that there can be no adultery or incest if there is no bodily contact between the man and the woman. Therefore, children born of such a process are legitimate.

This conclusion, according to Freehof, is based on a discussion in the Talmud in reference to Lev. 21:13–14, which declares that the High Priest may marry only a virgin. In the talmudic discussion of the practical implications of this law, we learn that, if a High Priest married a virgin but then discovered that, although still a virgin, she is pregnant, the child is legitimate. Ben Zoma is asked how is it possible that the wife of the High Priest could be pregnant and yet remain a virgin? He said that it was possible that she was impregnated in the bath. Rashi explains this answer as follows: "In a public bathhouse, some male bathers had emitted semen and later this young woman, bathing there, too, was impregnated by it." In other words, the absence of sexual contact renders the child legitimate in the case of a virgin.

But what if the host mother or the genetic mother is married to another man? Rabbi Zirelsohn considers the child to be a *mamzer*. Another scholar, however, considers this child a *safek* (possible or doubtful) *mamzer*. Still others who do not consider the process adulterous consider the child legitimate and not a *mamzer*.

There is yet another factor to be considered. Is the child commanded to honor the sperm donor as the father? Rabbenu Tam, a medieval commentator, said that, without the physical act, the child is not required to honor the father, but Rabbi Moshe Feinstein ruled that such honor is due.

WHAT IF THE HOST OR DONOR IS NOT JEWISH?

Another issue arises when either the host mother or the genetic mother is not Jewish. Is the child Jewish or not? Halachically, a child is Jewish if the mother is Jewish or the child is converted to Judaism.

In Orthodoxy, if the sperm from the prospective father is implanted in a non-Jewish woman, the baby is considered non-Jewish. If implanted into a Jewish woman, the child will be considered Jewish. The religion of the mother, not the father, determines the religion of the child resulting from the ovum.

In the case of in vitro fertilization of the wife's

egg by the husband's sperm, which is then carried to term by a surrogate, the question arises as to who is the real mother? Though there are differences of opinion, Rabbi Moshe Feinstein ruled that the child's religion follows that of the woman who carried it.

In Judaism, if the mother is Jewish and the father not Jewish, the child is considered Jewish. Within Reform Judaism, if the father is Jewish and the mother not Jewish, the child is presumed to be Jewish if that child is raised Jewishly.

A MORAL AND ETHICAL RESPONSE TO SURROGACY

But what about Baby M? Using the halachic ideas we have already considered, we could argue that there is no reason to reject the notion of surrogate parenthood. You might say that in some ways it is no different from adoption. Certainly it might be seen as no less permissible than any of the other new reproductive technologies. But surrogate mothering is qualitatively different from any of these, and it raises problems. In all the other technologies, the woman who will raise the child is helped to become pregnant. She carries it and gives birth to it. In most other technologies, the father who will raise the child is also the biological father. In one case—artificial insemination using donor sperm—the biological father is a stranger but not the mother.

In surrogate parenthood, however, the woman who carries the fetus and must then relinquish the newborn child bears additional burdens that give rise to moral and ethical dilemmas.

- The surrogacy arrangement does not adequately account for the health risks to which pregnant women are exposed or the bond that develops between the surrogate mother and the life growing within her womb.

- There is also the danger of economic and class exploitation. Already in the trial of Baby M, that question was raised. The practice of surrogate motherhood can create an incentive for economically deprived women to be exploited as "baby factories," which is contrary to our most fundamental Jewish values.

The chief rabbi of the British Empire, Immanuel Jakobovits, has stated: "To use another person as 'incubator' and take from her the child she carried and delivered, for a fee, is a revolting degradation of maternity and an affront to human dignity."

Other authorities, using Jewish law as a guide, do not accept the view that it is degrading to carry the child of another woman for a fee. Just as a physician is entitled to be compensated for time spent with the patient, they say, the woman is being compensated for her time in carrying and giving birth. There is no reason why a woman cannot be compensated for her time, her expenses, and even the physical risks that accompany pregnancy and childbirth.

Is the surrogacy contract Jewishly valid? That depends on the answers to the following questions:

1. Does it involve the sale of a human being?
2. Does Jewish law recognize such a contract as binding?

First, surrogacy does not involve the sale of a human being. The father can be viewed as compensating the mother for the time she carries the child. The child belongs to the father as well. He is not "buying" that which can be considered to be naturally his.

Second, a contract entered into in good faith is a valid contract. Some rabbis regard it as invalid because it pertains to something not yet "in the world." Others insist the contract begins to take effect when the fertilized egg enters the surrogate mother's womb.

Such halachic differences should not blur the fact that modern technology has given infertile couples new hope. At the same time we must be careful to employ modern techologies in ways that do not compromise or degrade our humanity. Our halachic tradition allows Jews to take advantage of advances in science, confident that we can be partners with God in helping people like Michael's parents experience the joy of bringing children into the world.

MICHAEL AND HIS RABBI

After a long talk with his rabbi, Michael, who had been conceived through artificial insemination, felt more comfortable about his manner of birth and about his Jewish status. There never had been the slightest question of whether or not he "really" was Jewish.

CHAPTER
5

TO TELL THE TRUTH:
Do Cheaters Ever Prosper?

Josh Greenberg was having a bad day. Things were getting more than a little out of control in his life. He had some tough decisions to make. To find relief, Josh passed some time in the school library. Leafing through the newspaper, he spotted an item on the editorial page. A rabbi was analyzing the high incidence of Jewish involvement in illegal Wall Street "insider trading" schemes:

Jews are uncomfortable reading about other Jews who have committed white collar crimes. . . . The large number of scandals involving Jews suggests that the religious institutions of America have failed to instill in their followers the values of honesty and integrity.

To Josh it read:

Jews are uncomfortable reading about the Josh Greenbergs of our society who steal answer sheets for their final exams in order to score better grades, get into the college of their choice, and live happily ever after. . . .

Josh's problem began when, stopping by the school office between classes, he stumbled upon a copy of the answer sheet for his math final. Without even thinking about what he was doing,

Josh slid the sheet into his notebook. Now here he was, sitting in the library, concealing stolen property. His head pounding, he contemplated his next move.

- Look at it right now?
- Carry it around the rest of the day and study it when he got home?
- Throw it away without looking at it?
- Surrender himself to the principal and confess?
- Sell the answers and make a profit in addition to scoring an A?
- Slide it secretly back into the place where he found it?

Sitting there in the agony of indecision, Josh noticed a book on a nearby shelf: *Jewish Ethics: An Everyday Guide*. Was he hallucinating? No, it looked real enough. He got up, took down the book, and opened it, finding information that helped him eventually solve his dilemma.

THE ETHICS OF HONESTY

The Spanish author Cervantes once wrote: "Honesty is the best policy." And the British essayist Alexander Pope said: "An honest man is the noblest work of God." But long before these writers were even born, Jewish tradition recognized the value of honesty as a means of assuring a good and productive life.

The rabbis considered honesty one of the requirements for entry into the world to come. In the Talmud, "Raba said: When man is led in for judgment [in the next world], he is asked: Did you deal faithfully [i.e., with integrity]?"

Rabbi Simeon ben Gamaliel said: "On three things the world rests: on justice, on truth, and on peace. And all three are contained in the teachings of the prophet Zechariah, who said: 'These are the things that you shall do: Speak you every man the truth with his neighbor; execute the judgment of truth and peace in your gates . . .' [8:16] And the three are one. If there is truth there is peace; where there is justice, peace and truth are present also."

The rabbis divided honesty and integrity into two categories: (1) the relationship between people and God (bein adam lamakom) and (2) the relationship between one person and another (bein adam lechavero). Relations between one person and another were deemed critical. In fact, so sensitive were the rabbis to the feelings of people, they declared that, if a person wronged somebody and did not personally ask forgiveness, even atonement on Yom Kippur would not "clear the slate." Fasting and praying on Yom Kippur help when a person sins against God but not against another human being: "Thus did Rabbi Eleazar ben Azariah declare, 'From all your sins before the Eternal shall you be clean.'" (Lev. 16:30). In other words, the Day of Atonement achieves forgiveness for transgressions by people toward God. But for transgressions between people, Yom Kippur does not effect atonement until they first make peace between themselves. (Talmud)

TAKING BRIBES

Dishonesty takes many forms, among them the taking of bribes—"Do not take bribes; for bribes blind the clear-sighted and upset the pleas of the just." (Exod. 23:8) The Book of Deuteronomy also emphasizes the prohibition against taking bribes. "You shall not wrest judgment; you shall not respect persons [favor the rich and powerful]; neither shall you take a gift [bribe]; for a gift blinds the eyes of the wise, and perverts the words of the righteous." (16:19)

The rabbis recognized that bribery can take many forms. The Talmud describes a situation in which even shaking a judge's hand was considered bribery. The judge Samuel was once crossing (a river) on a ferry when a man came up and began to shake his hand. "What is your business here?" asked Samuel. "I have a lawsuit," answered the man. "I see," said Samuel. "In that case, I am disqualified from the suit."

BEARING FALSE WITNESS

Dishonesty also takes the forms of perjury and bearing false witness: ". . . if the witness is a false witness, and has testified falsely against his brother; then shall you do unto him, as he had purposed to do unto his brother; so shall you put away the evil from the midst of you." (Deut. 19:18,19) In Leviticus, God declares: "You shall not swear falsely by My name, profaning the name of your God: I am the Lord." (19:12)

SPREADING GOSSIP

You don't have to be in a court of law to harm someone by bearing false witness. Equally contemptible and condemned in the Torah (Exod. 23:1) are gossip and the spreading of ugly rumors, in Hebrew leshon hara (an evil tongue). Jewish tradition teaches that this kind of slander offends God, for it cruelly destroys people's reputations.

The Talmud declares: "Four classes of men will never see God's face—the scoffer, the liar, the slanderer, and the hypocrite."

The rabbis taught: "Greater is the sin of the evil tongue than the sin of idolatry."

The *Zohar* states: "God accepts repentance for all sins, except the sin of imposing a bad name upon another."

In the Talmud we read, "Slander injures three persons: the slanderer, the one who listens to the slander, and the person slandered."

The tongue has the power to condemn or to comfort: "Rabban Simeon ben Gamaliel commanded his slave Tabbai to buy the best food in the market. The slave brought home a cow's tongue. The next day Rabban Simeon ben Gamaliel commanded him to buy the worst thing in the market and again Tabbai brought home tongue. When asked for an explanation, the wise slave replied: There is nothing better than a good tongue, and nothing worse than an evil tongue." (Midrash)

CHEATING

Just as one can lie with words, one can also lie with deeds, such as plagiarism or cheating on tests.

The rabbis of the Talmud were unequivocal in their condemnation of cheating. "Samuel said: One must not 'steal the mind' of one's fellow man." In another talmudic tractate, Rabbi Simeon ben Yochai taught that "to deceive with words [or abuse with the tongue] is a greater offense than to cheat in monetary matters."

THEFT

The most tangible expression of dishonesty is the violation of another's property rights, such as thievery. The Bible commands repeatedly: "You shall not steal." (Exod. 20:13) When a theft took place in ancient times, restitution in the form of monetary compensation (punishment in kind) was imposed upon the offender.

Real estate theft—by removing boundary stones of a neighbor's property to increase your own—was also strictly prohibited: "You shall not remove your neighbor's landmark . . . in the land that the Lord your God gives you." (Deut. 19:14)

FRAUD

Defrauding customers by using false weights and measures or other methods of deception constitutes yet another breach of honesty. In Leviticus 19:35–36 we read: "You shall do no unrighteousness in judgment, . . . in weight, or in measure. Just balances [and] just weights . . . shall you have. I am the Lord your God." Deuteronomy 25:15–16 promises long life as the reward for honesty: "A perfect and just weight you shall have; a perfect and just measure . . . that your days may be long upon the land which the Lord your God gives you."

LIVE WITH SELF-RESPECT

We have discussed the requirements of honesty and integrity in terms of what one should *not* do. What positive steps can be taken to reinforce one's self-esteem? How can you live your life to enhance self-respect?

The Hebrew prophet Micah proclaimed: "[God] has told you . . . what is good, and what the Lord requires of you: only to do justice and to love goodness and to walk modestly with your God." (6:8) The rabbis in the Talmud felt that being honorable was so crucial that the first question God asks one when one appears before the heavenly throne is "Were you honorable? Did you deal faithfully [i.e., with integrity] . . . ?" *Pirkei Avot* (The Ethics of the Fathers) is succinct, practical, and to the point: "Which is the right path that a person should choose? That which is honorable in itself and wins honor from others." (2:1) A person should go so far in maintaining personal dignity as to even avoid hearing evil. The Talmud captures the essence of how to avoid evil by relating a statement by Rabbi Eleazar: "Why do the fingers of human beings resemble pegs . . . ? The reason is that if people hear unworthy things they should plug their fingers into their ears."

CHOOSING THE RIGHT FRIENDS

The rabbis understood that personal honesty and integrity could be affected by our friends. Peer pressure, then as now, was hard to resist. The rabbis, therefore, cautioned against having the wrong sorts of friends:

> Be aware that the companionship of the ungodly is obnoxious, that their example surrounds us like the plague. Enter not into the path of the wicked! (Prov. 4:14) Loiter not in the streets, sit not in the highway, go not with those whose society is discreditable. As the sages say: "One that walks with wise men shall be wise" (Prov. 13:20), and Ben Mishle writes: Choose upright people for friends. With them take counsel, but despise fools! With the wise you can overturn a rock. And find safety against giants' rage!
> (*Hebrew Ethical Wills*, selected and edited by Israel Abrahams, Jewish Publication Society, 1948, p. 63)

The reward of honesty is honesty itself and the respect of friends, family, and colleagues.

THE LIMITS OF TRUTH

Must we always tell the truth, no matter what the consequences, or is it permissible at times to tell a "white lie"? Are there times when not telling the truth is the proper course of action?

In Judaism, if telling a falsehood serves to help people, encourage them, enhance their lives, or bring about peace, then it is permissible. Aaron, brother of Moses, is known in the *Ethics of the Fathers* as a *rodef shalom*, a pursuer of peace, in part because he stretched the truth. It is told that two friends once became angry with each other. Aaron went to each of them and said, "Your friend is very sorry for having quarreled with you in so angry a manner. The next time he sees you he will apologize." Aaron had in fact made up the whole scenario. But the next time the two men met, they embraced and apologized to each other, reaffirming their friendship.

You may also build others' self-confidence by telling them that they are beautiful or wonderful, even though it may not be absolutely true. We are told that in the communities of Eastern Europe it was the custom that one should "dance before the bride" and describe her as beautiful and graceful, even if she was not. In other words, embellishing the truth in the performance of a mitzvah is permissible.

YOUR ANSWER

Take a minute and reflect about all that Josh learned.

Before we tell you what Josh did, what would you do if a fellow student offered you the answers to tomorrow's math final. Write your answer.

WHAT JOSH DID

By the time Josh finished reading the book it was fairly clear what he should do. He came to understand that his own sense of integrity—his self-respect—was worth more than a grade on any exam and more than anybody else's admiration. Even if he were the only one who knew what he did, his knowledge that he had done the wrong thing would give him a greater sense of failure than a low grade in a course.

Fortunately, Josh had not looked at the answer sheet. Should he tell the teacher that he had found the answer sheet but had not looked at it? He would sleep on that question. Perhaps in the morning he would know whether to take that extra step or not.

But he knew what to do right now. He reached his hand into his notebook and found the answer sheet. Slowly and deliberately he crumpled it up into a little ball. On his way out of the library he aimed it at the librarian's trash can. Basket!

CHAPTER
6

ABORTION:
Is a Fetus a Human Being?

Linda's older sister, Joan, was pregnant, and Linda was very worried. Joan, twenty-six years old and unmarried, had told Linda that she intended to have an abortion. Joan's doctor had agreed to perform the abortion at a local clinic and assured her that there was little medical risk.

Still, Linda was upset. Even though she was only sixteen, she had read one article after another in newspapers and magazines, condemning abortion as "a sin," "murder," and "the taking of innocent life." The Pope insisted that there were no circumstances under which abortion could be condoned. And Linda was aware that many court cases were pending in states across the country that could further limit or reverse the U.S. Supreme Court's 1973 ruling (*Roe* v. *Wade*), which had affirmed the right of a woman to have her pregnancy medically terminated.

Linda had heard her rabbi strongly advocate the right of a woman to have an abortion as a matter of choice. What she desperately wanted to know was whether this was just a personal opinion on her rabbi's part or whether there were any circumstances in which Jewish tradition permitted abortion. She called Rabbi Levine

and made an appointment to see her. Linda listened very carefully as the rabbi explained.

IN THE TORAH

According to Jewish law, the fetus is not a living being, i.e., it is not technically a human person until the moment of birth. Therefore, the Jewish legal tradition does not view abortion as murder. The basis for this view is biblical. In the Book of Exodus, we read:

> When men fight, and one of them pushes a pregnant woman and a miscarriage results, but no other damage ensues, the one responsible shall be *fined*. . . . But if other damage ensues, the penalty shall be life for life. . . .
>
> (21:22)

The law here is quite clear: the penalty for aborting the fetus is monetary compensation. This implies that murder was not committed and hence the fetus is not regarded as a person. But in causing the death of the woman, murder was committed and the punishment was death. This view of the status of the fetus and the consequent attitude toward abortion is emphasized in both the *Mishnah* and the *Gemara*.

IN THE MISHNAH

The *Mishnah* states that, if a woman is having difficulty in giving birth, it is permitted to remove surgically the child from inside her womb [even if that causes death to the child] and take it out because her life takes precedence. However, if the greater part of the child has come out, it must not be touched because one life must not be taken to save another.

Thus, to save the life of the mother the fetus may be destroyed, up until the time it leaves the womb. A child who has emerged from the womb, however, may not be harmed in any way—even to save the life of the mother.

Human life is sacred and murder is absolutely prohibited. If Judaism took the view that destroying a fetus constituted homicide, abortions for any reason would not be permissible in Jewish law. If Jewish law had recognized the fetus as a human life, we would have been confronted with a painful dilemma in cases in which continuing a pregnancy endangered the woman's life, having to choose between saving one human life at the expense of another.

THE RABBINIC COMMENTATORS

Rashi (1040–1105), one of the foremost commentators on the Bible and Talmud, summarizes the passage we looked at in the *Mishnah* as follows:

As long as the child has not entered into the world, it is not called a living being, and it is therefore permissible to take its life in order to save the life of its mother. Once the head of the child has come out, the child may not be harmed because it is considered as fully born, and one life may not be taken to save another.

Maimonides (1135–1204) explains that the fetus may be aborted if it is threatening the life of the mother: ". . . when a woman has difficulty in giving birth, one may remove the child in her womb—either with drugs or by surgery—because it is like a pursuer trying to kill her . . ." Virtually all rabbinic authorities agree that, until the fetus has emerged, it may be destroyed if it is threatening the life of its mother, even in the last stage of pregnancy.

The great scholar Rabbi Jacob Emden went even further, arguing that it was permissible to perform an abortion in the case of "great need," as long as the birth process had not yet begun. In elaborating on what he considered "great need," Emden said it would suffice even if the reason *is not to save the mother's life—even if it is only to save her from the "great* [psychological] *pain" it* [the pregnancy] *causes her.*

Underlying these laws and decisions is a concern for the welfare and well-being of the woman. Rabbi Solomon B. Freehof, a great liberal modern authority and interpreter of Jewish law, pointed out that a fetus has no independent life and, just as a person may sacrifice a part of herself, such as an arm or a leg, to be cured of a more severe illness, so may a woman sacrifice this part of herself. For Rabbi Freehof and others, the fetus is important as *potential* human life, but its claims are secondary to those of a human person who already exists—namely the mother.

Abortion, then, is morally permissible in Jewish law and may even be morally necessary. In fact, according to some authorities, if a woman's life is threatened by childbirth, the fetus *must* be aborted. The woman may not even have the option of choosing to die for the sake of giving birth to the child.

It is worthwhile noting that the U.S. Supreme Court in the historic *Roe* v. *Wade* and *Doe* v. *Bolton* decisions had expressed a position very similar to that of Jewish law:

The Constitution does not define "person" in so many words. The use of the word is such that it has application only postnatally. The unborn have never been recognized in law as persons in the whole sense.

The Orthodox rabbinate today takes a much more stringent view of the Jewish legal position on abortion, limiting it to special cases, as when a woman is impregnated through rape or incest, or when it is clear that continuation of the pregnancy to birth could constitute a clear danger to the life or health of the mother. Nevertheless, most Conservative and Reform rabbis, drawing from the same long legal tradition, take the more liberal stance of permitting abortion, if determined advisable by a woman in consultation with her physician.

IS ABORTION MURDER?

Is abortion murder? The rabbis of the Talmud in discussing the question "When does the soul enter the fetus?" proposed various answers: perhaps the soul enters at the moment of conception, or perhaps at circumcision, or perhaps at birth, or perhaps when the child is able to say Amen.

But the rabbis set aside the question of "ensoulment," because it intruded into "the secrets of God." Though Judaism *deals* with the theological question as to whether or not a soul enters a fetus, its primary interest is with the *human* question: "Is abortion murder?" The rabbis answered emphatically and unequivocally no, as the following examples illustrate:

1. In the case of a pregnant mother who has been told that the continuation of her pregnancy would dilute the milk with which she is nursing another infant, Jewish law permits abortion to protect the welfare of the existing nursing child.
2. Tay-Sachs disease is a genetic illness that particularly affects Jewish infants. No Tay-Sachs child has ever lived beyond five years of age. Such children die an agonizing death. During pregnancy, Tay-Sachs disease cannot be detected until the second trimester. In spite of this, Jewish law permits therapeutic abortion even at this late date.

Dr. David M. Feldman, a Conservative rabbi and a recognized expert in this field of Jewish law, states:

The rights of the fetus, therefore, are quite secondary to the rights of the mother. *She* is a living human person *now;* the *fetus* is not yet a human person. The slogan we hear nowadays, *"right to life,"* confuses this principle. When we are speaking about abortion, the issue is not at all "right to life," but rather "right to be born." It must be stated that in Jewish law there exists *no right to be born, only a right to life of persons who already exist.* The use of the word "persons" here is also important. Those who oppose abortion point to evidence that life begins early in the fetal stage. Yes, life may begin early, but our question still has to be: What kind of life? *There is human life, animal life, plant life. The distinction has to be made between life and human life.* Rabbinic law has determined *that human life begins with birth.*

IN SUMMARY

According to Jewish law, a fetus is potential life. It becomes human life only when it is born. And it is precisely because of the regard for the sanctity of life that at least the liberal wings of the Jewish community affirm the right of any woman to freely choose whether to have an abortion or to give birth.

LINDA'S LETTER

Linda left the rabbi's office with a great sense of relief. Just knowing that Jewish tradition allowed for elective abortion alleviated much of the uneasiness she had felt about her sister's decision. It occurred to her that Joan might be asking herself exactly the same questions that Linda had raised with Rabbi Levine. Perhaps she felt a bit guilty about having an abortion, and perhaps knowing what Judaism had to say would be important to her.

Therefore, Linda decided to write Joan a letter, sharing what she had learned.

Write the letter you think Linda might have sent to her sister.

A FINAL WORD

There are certain matters on which the major religious traditions disagree. Abortion is one of those difficult issues. While we respect the beliefs of others, we as liberal Jews have our own traditions and practices that are just as precious to us. The right of a woman to free choice in the matter of abortion is one of *our* values, one we affirm with deep conviction.

Even if there are sectors of the Jewish community that take a more stringent attitude toward abortion, we are absolutely certain that this question is, in the end, a matter of conscience, to be decided by the woman, not the state.

CHAPTER
7

WAR AND PEACE:
Is War Always Wrong?

Danny was confused—confused and embarrassed. While attending the national board meeting of the North American Federation of Temple Youth, he got himself into an unlikely dispute with one of the great teachers of Reform Judaism—a professor at the Hebrew Union College-Jewish Institute of Religion and an outstanding spokesman for social justice and peace. Danny thought of himself as deeply committed to the prophetic values of the Reform movement, but something the professor said disturbed and confused him.

The professor had remarked that a peace-loving Jew would never engage in violence, would never pick up a weapon. On hearing this, Danny blurted out, "But what about the Jewish heroes of the Warsaw Ghetto who rose up against the Nazis? They took up arms for self-preservation and to defend Jewish honor." The professor replied, "Better they should have died without blood on their hands than to pick up rifles and take other lives."

The exchange left Danny unsure of Judaism's teachings on war and peace. Do you agree with Danny or with the pacifist professor?

YOUR ANSWER FIRST

Jewish tradition has a lot to say on this subject. But before you examine the literature, write what you imagine to be the Jewish position. After you read this chapter, compare your answer with the answer offered by Jewish tradition.

JEWISH SOURCES

During worship services, Danny paid particular attention to the prayers. Some of them could not help but leap out at him. He read:

> Grant us peace, Your most precious gift, O Eternal Source of peace, and give us the will to proclaim its message to all the peoples of the earth. Bless our country, that it may always be a stronghold of peace, and its advocate among the nations. May contentment reign within its borders, health and happiness within its homes. Strengthen the bonds of friendship among the inhabitants of all lands. And may the love of Your name hallow every home and every heart. Blessed is the Eternal God, the Source of peace.

Rabbi Geller blessed the congregation, ending with the words: "May the Lord lift up His countenance upon you, and give you peace." The longing for peace ran like a thread through the entire service.

Later, Danny told Rabbi Geller about the encounter at the NFTY board meeting and asked if Judaism was essentially pacifist.

Rabbi Geller told Danny to consult the Bible and suggested certain specific passages. "You may be surprised at what you will find," the rabbi cautioned.

Danny learned that the *Tanach* seemed to accept war as a fact of life. Even Abraham played the role of warrior—and very successfully. (Gen. 14:2ff.) The Bible is filled with accounts of battles: God defeats Pharaoh's army at the Red Sea (Exod. 14:1–31); Moses leads the Jews in battle against the Amalekites (Exod. 17:8–16); Joshua leads the people against the Canaanite nations (Joshua 17:18ff.); Deborah is both a prophet and a warrior, personally leading the charge against the armies of Sisera (Judges 4); Saul and David both become king by virtue of their ability to mount successful battles against the Philistines (I Samuel 19:8, 14:47); and so on.

Throughout the Jewish Bible, war heroes seem to be admired and glorified. People identified as prophets are depicted as favoring war. Deborah urges Barak to make war on Sisera (Judges 4:6ff.); Elisha urges the king of Israel, Joash, to go to war with Syria (II Kings 13:14–19); King Ahab is urged to go to battle with Ben-hadad by an anonymous "prophet" (I Kings 20:13–14); and the prophet Joel, whose words are recorded in a book of the *Tanach* that bears his name, says, "Proclaim you this among the nations, prepare war; stir up the mighty men; let all the men of war draw near, let them come up. Beat your plowshares into swords, and your pruning-hooks into spears. . . ." (Joel 4:9–10)

Perhaps most surprising of all, God is depicted as a warrior. Right after the Jewish people had successfully evaded the Egyptian armies and crossed the Red Sea, they sang an exultant song of victory, proclaiming, "The Lord is a man

of war, the Lord is His name. . . . Your right hand, O Lord . . . dashes in pieces the enemy. . . ." (Exod. 15:3,6) This idea is even elaborated upon by later Jewish tradition. One rabbinic discussion notes an apparent contradiction between a verse in the Book of Daniel and a verse in the Song of Songs. In one verse it is written:

> His raiment was as white snow, and the hair of his head like pure wool. (Dan. 7:9) But [elsewhere] it says, "His locks are curled, and black as a raven." (Song of Songs 5:11) There is no contradiction. This verse (i.e., Daniel) refers to God as sitting in judgment, and the other one (Song of Songs) refers to God during times of war. For as one rabbi said, "In sitting in judgment no one is more appropriate than an old man, and in war, no one is more appropriate than a young man."　　　　(Talmud)

The *Tanach* portrays religious people consulting with God prior to engaging in battle. The High Priest at times would put on his ritual garb and stand before the ark, as the soldiers prepared themselves. Battles often began with sacrifices offered to God or with a fasting period.

It seems that every Jewish army had a "chaplain"—a priest who accompanied the soldiers into battle. Phinehas served this function during the Exodus when the Jewish people went to battle against the Midianites. (Num. 31:6) One portion of Deuteronomy suggests that a priest's duties included caring for the spiritual welfare of the soldiers and inspiring them before the attack. (Deut. 20:2–4) The shofar, which we identify today with such holy times as Rosh Hashanah and Yom Kippur, once was employed to assemble the troops and to sound the attack. At times the High Priest, while accompanying the troops into battle, carried the Holy Ark, just as pagan armies brought idols onto the battlefield. The Talmud requires that the king carry a *Sefer Torah* in leading the army into battle. All this hardly sounds like the writings of a tradition fundamentally opposed to warfare.

Although warfare evidently was accepted as a fact of life, Jewish law placed significant restrictions on how war was to be conducted. Often ambassadors were called upon to negotiate disputes in an attempt to avoid war. (Judges 11: 12–28; I Samuel 11:1–10; I Kings 20:2–11) Israelites were forbidden to attack unless they first issued a demand that the enemy surrender. (Deut. 20:10ff.). When Israelites besieged a city, they were forbidden to cut down the fruit trees of that city:

> When you shall besiege a city a long time, in making war against it to take it, you shall not destroy the trees thereof by wielding an axe against them; for you may eat of them, but you shall not cut them down; for is the tree of the field man, that it should be besieged of you? Only the trees of which you know that they are not trees for food, them you may destroy. . . .　　　　(Deuteronomy 20:19–20)

Maimonides carries this prohibition even further:

> When siege is laid to a city for the purpose of capture, it may not be surrounded on all four sides, but only on three in order to give an opportunity for escape to those who would flee to save their lives.

Though it was customary in the ancient Near East for triumphant armies to take prisoners, the Torah was insistent that Jewish soldiers show a proper respect for the human feeling of women who became their captives. (Deut. 21:10–14) The rabbis even limited war by deeming it a violation to bear arms on Shabbat, though later laws amended this law in special circumstances.

In the ancient Near East, where warfare was a common occurrence, not all Jews were obligated to participate in battle. The twentieth chapter of Deuteronomy clearly exempts significant categories of men from the battlefield: one who has built a house but not moved into it; one who has planted a vineyard but not consumed its fruit; one who is betrothed but not yet married; or even one who is "fearful and faint-hearted." (Deut. 20:5–8)

Later rabbis identified different types of war:

the obligatory war (*milchemet mitzvah*, or *milchemet chovah*) and the voluntary war (*milchemet reshut*). Israelites were obliged to combat the seven nations that inhabited Canaan, the great enemy Amalek, and those who attacked an Israelite city. These priority wars sanctioned a broad range of actions. In contrast, voluntary wars, those waged for the purpose of extending Jewish territory, were restricted. Such wars could be declared only by the full Sanhedrin, a sort of Jewish Supreme Court in ancient times, consisting of seventy-one members. In such a voluntary war, military exemptions were much easier to obtain.

Jewish tradition has never glorified militarism. Indeed, the rabbis elevated peace to one of Judaism's highest values. Throughout the *Tanach*, we read such words as "And I will give peace in the land, and you shall lie down, and none shall make you afraid . . . neither shall the sword go through your land" (Lev. 26:6); "The Lord will give strength unto His people; the Lord will bless His people with peace" (Psalms 29:11); "Depart from evil, and do good; seek peace, and pursue it." (Psalms 34:15)

Perhaps no evocation of peace in all of human literature is more famous, or beloved, than the words of Isaiah:

> And it shall come to pass in the end of days . . . that they shall beat their swords into plowshares, and their spears into pruning-hooks; nation shall not lift up sword against nation, neither shall they learn war any more.
>
> (2:2,4)

King David, perhaps the greatest military leader of the ancient kingdom of Israel, was denied the honor of building the Temple specifically because he had spilled so much blood in warfare. Instead, God chose David's son Solomon to erect the holy structure. (I Chron. 22:7–10)

In later tradition, the rabbis viewed Aaron as the personification of peace: "Hillel used to say: 'Be of the disciples of Aaron, loving peace and pursuing peace.'" (*Pirkei Avot* 1:12) The rabbis taught that Aaron "loved peace and pursued peace and made peace between one person and another, as it is written: 'the law of truth was in his mouth, and unrighteousness was not found in his lips; he walked with Me in peace and uprightness, and did turn many away from iniquity.' " (Malachi 2:6 and Talmud)

If interpersonal peace was a goal that people should seek in their own lives, by extension peace between nations was an absolute goal. The Talmud teaches that to achieve peace, one could even "blot out God's name," or lie.

"Great is peace, for all blessings are contained in it. . . . Great is peace, for God's name is peace. . . ." In the Midrash we read:

> Seek peace, and pursue it." (Psalms 34:15) The Lord does not command you to run after or pursue the other commandments, but merely to fulfill them only upon the appropriate occasion. But peace you must seek in your own place and pursue it even to another place as well.

Peace is equal to all of creation. Without peace there is nothing. Human beings are called on to work for peace, and to pray for peace. "Rabbah, son of R. Shila, said [that] 'a man should pray for peace even until the last clod of earth [is thrown upon his grave].' "

The talmudic sage Rab would conclude his prayers by asking God to grant a long life, a good life, a life of blessing, and a life of peace. This prayer is now one that is regularly said on the Shabbat on which the new moon is announced.

God is understood as granting peace. Job says that God "makes peace in His high places." (Job 25:1) To the rabbis this meant that God built peace and harmony into the very pattern of creation, and so would God build harmony into human life. As Rabban Simeon, the son of Gamaliel, used to say, "On three things does the world stand: on justice, on truth, and on peace." (*Pirkei Avot* 1:18)

The traditional worship service has as its center the *Amidah*, nineteen blessings, one of which begins with the words "Grant peace, goodness, blessing, grace, love, and mercy to us and to all the households of Israel." The blessing concludes, "May it please You to bless Your people Israel at every season and at all times with Your peace. Praised are you, O Lord, who blesses Your people with peace."

Jewish tradition teaches us to look realistically at our world. The nations of the world are not immune to war and aggression. Perhaps there is "a time to love, and a time to hate; a time for war, and a time for peace." (Ecclesiastes 3:8) But the ideal remains that loftier vision held out by Isaiah: "The work of righteousness shall be peace, and the effect of righteousness quietness and security forever." (32:17)

When the Jewish people dreams its collective dream, it looks forward to that time of perfect peace. At the end of each Shabbat, and in the midst of every Pesach seder, we look forward to the arrival of Elijah, the forerunner of the Messiah, the messenger who declares the coming of perfect peace. As God has promised, "Behold, I will send you Elijah the prophet . . ." (Malachi 3:23) Our tradition understands that it is of him that Isaiah says, "How beautiful upon the mountains are the feet of the messenger . . . that announces peace. . . ." (Isaiah 52:7)

Peace seems ever on our minds. When traditional Jews greet one another, for example, they say, *Shalom Aleichem*—peace be with you. And, at the most precious moments of our lives, when we are blessed, it is always with the words Danny heard Rabbi Geller say on that Shabbat: "The Lord lift up His countenance upon you, and give you peace." (Num. 6:26)

Does Jewish tradition teach pacifism? No, not literally. But then again, there is surely room for such a stance within a tradition that would express itself in terms of a prayer attributed to Rabbi Nachman of Bratslav:

> May it be Your will, Lord our God and God of our ancestors, Master of peace, King who possesses peace, to grant peace to Your people Israel. And may that peace increase until it extends to all who inhabit the world, so there is no hatred, jealousy, strife, triumphalism, or reproach between one person and another, so that only love and peace will embrace them all.

CHAPTER
8

OBEDIENCE TO PARENTS:
When Is It Permissible to Disobey?

In all his years on the bench, Judge Shapero had never had a case like this. A high school computer whiz admitted stealing hundreds of dollars worth of long distance phone calls. It seemed like an open-and-shut case, but the computer genius pleaded not guilty, telling Judge Shapero: "I am fulfilling a more important obligation—honoring my parents." It turned out that the whole scheme was the idea of his father, who, lacking computer skills, enlisted his son as an accomplice.

Judge Shapero was outraged at the defendant's response. Before handing down a stiff legal penalty, however, the judge decided to determine if Jewish tradition actually sanctioned blind allegiance to a parent's illegal demands. The judge phoned Rabbi Cook for an opinion.

JEWISH SOURCES

The rabbis taught that three partners create a human being: God, the father, and the mother.
(Talmud)

That is the principle upon which the Jewish understanding of the parent-child relationship rests. Children must respect their parents, who are considered partners with God in the rearing of children: "The Holy One, blessed be He, says, 'I ascribe [merit] to . . . [the parents] as though I myself had come to dwell among them, and they had honored me.'" The idea of honoring parents, as we all know, is one of the Ten Commandments:

Honor your father and your mother, that you may long endure on the land which the Lord your God is giving you.   (Exodus 20:12)

Honor your father and your mother, as the Lord your God has commanded you, that you may long endure, and that you may fare well, in the land that the Lord your God is giving you.   (Deuteronomy 5:16)

When the verse in Deuteronomy is discussed in the Talmud, the rabbis explain the words "that you may long endure, and that you may fare well" in economic terms: ". . . a person enjoys the interest in this world and the principal in the world to come."

Elsewhere in the Torah, we are commanded, "You shall revere everyone his mother and his father." (Lev. 19:3) "Honoring" parents is equated with revering God ("Revere only the

Lord your God and worship Him alone"). (Deut. 6:13)

We read in the Talmud a compelling story about the measure of honor a child is expected to give parents:

> Rabbi Eleazer was asked, "To what extent is honoring one's father and mother to be practiced?" He answered, "Go forth and see how a certain non-Jew from Ashkelon, Dama, the son of Nathina by name, acted toward his father. He was approached about selling precious stones . . . at a profit of 600,000 denari; but the keys [to the vault containing the gems] were lying under his father's pillow. The son refused to disturb his father's sleep."

The Talmud gives another example of just how far a child could go in honoring parents:

> Rabbi Abbahu tells the story about his son, Abimi, whom he asked to bring him a glass of water. By the time the son brought it to him, the father had fallen asleep. Therefore, the son bent and stood over him until he woke.

We also have stories of great men honoring their mothers:

> Rabbi Tarfon had a mother for whom, whenever she would want to climb into bed, he would bend down and let her ascend by stepping on him.

> Whenever Rabbi Joseph heard his mother's footsteps, he would say, "Arise before the approaching *Shechinah* [the presence of God]."

The rabbis understood that even more important than the actions we take in honoring our parents is the *intent* of those actions, the attitudes that underlie behavior. One talmudic scholar said that it is possible to give your parents exotic and expensive food yet have this be a shameful act, whereas another person could force the parents to operate the grindstone in a mill and still have this be considered virtuous. How could this be so? A story is told of a man who "once fed his father pheasants." When his father asked him how he could afford them, he answered, "What business is it of yours, old man . . . eat!" On another occasion it happened that the father of a man who operated a grinding stone was drafted into the army. The son said to his father, "Serving in the army is very dangerous. You take my job in the mill and I will take your place in the army."

Jewish tradition holds that children must respect their parents when they are alive and after they die—making funeral arrangements, saying *Kaddish* for up to twelve months, remembering them on their *yahrzeits* (the anniversaries of their deaths), and observing all the rites of mourning and remembrance. The Talmud says that, whenever children speak of deceased parents, they are to say, "May their memory be for a blessing."

What does a child do when parents are wrong? There are times when a child is expected to correct parents, but it must be done gently and politely. The Talmud teaches that, if one's father is (unwittingly) violating a teaching of the Torah, one must not say to him, "Father, you violated a biblical teaching," but rather, "Father, isn't this what the Torah says?"

There are even times when children are *allowed* to disobey parents, though tradition tries to limit such occasions:

> Eleazar ben Mathia said: "If my father orders, 'Give me a drink of water' while I have a mitzvah to perform, I disregard my father's honor and perform the mitzvah, since both my father and I are bound to fulfill the mitzvot." Issi ben Judah maintains: "If the mitzvah can be performed by others, it should be performed by others. . . ." The *halachah* is according to Issi ben Judah. (Talmud)

However, there are times when a child is *required* to disobey parents. Parents are not allowed to request or expect their children to violate the laws of Torah. If a parent tells a child to violate a religious law, therefore, the child is not obligated to obey the parent, for the child would be violating a higher law. The rabbis based their decision upon the *two* commandments combined in Leviticus 19:3—"You shall revere everyone his mother and his father, *and* keep My sabbaths: I the Lord am your God." Clearly it is the duty of parents and children to honor God. According to the Talmud, if a parent tells a child to act in violation of Torah and the child consents (by stealing, for example), the child is violating God's law, one that *both* parents and children are obligated to obey. Thus, the child in such a situation must not honor parents.

YOUR ANSWER

Before we share Judge Shapero's decision with you, write what you think the judge's decision should have been.

JUDGE SHAPERO'S DECISION

The young man owed his father respect and honor, but only to a point. Once the guilty father had crossed the line of decent and moral behavior, the son was not obligated to follow him; indeed, he was duty-bound to disobey. The son's loyalty was misplaced; so, too, was his sense of duty.

Judge Shapero took this into account when he pronounced sentence upon the young man, imposing a large fine and probation instead of a prison term. More than to punish the young man, he wanted to teach him and his father a lesson neither would forget.

CHAPTER
9

INDEPENDENCE V. DEPENDENCE:
Are Parents Always Right?

Rebecca was angry that Thursday afternoon at Hebrew school, and she didn't bother to hide it. She screamed at her parents from the temple's public telephone, accusing them of being unfair, uncaring, and cruel.

Rabbi Cohen overheard Rebecca's side of the phone conversation and was disturbed by the scene. When Rebecca slammed down the phone, he asked if she would like to speak with him. Reluctantly she agreed to step into his office. The rabbi asked Rebecca what was troubling her. Words came rushing out in no logical order. What Rabbi Cohen could piece together went something like this: Rebecca was captain of her soccer team, which in three days, next Sunday morning, was to compete in a championship match. Her parents insisted that she attend religious school, so, rather than being on the field, she would be at the temple, learning things she didn't care about and that made little sense to her. Finally, she asked, "Rabbi, do my parents have any right to force me to be here against my will?"

What gives our parents the right to make us do whatever they want? Rabbi Cohen spoke to Rebecca for a long time, explaining Jewish teachings about what it means to be a parent and how parents should treat their children. Then he answered her question. Can you guess what he said? You will find his explanation at the end of the chapter. First, consider some Jewish thoughts about the nature of parenthood and the responsibilities of parents.

Judaism regards parenthood as a mitzvah. In the very first commandment of the Torah God says to Adam and Eve: "Be fruitful, and multiply, and replenish the earth, and subdue it. . . ." (Gen. 1:28) In other words, the Torah teaches that it is a Jewish obligation to have children.

Jewish tradition looks upon children as the greatest joy in a parent's life. The Psalmist says, "Lo, children are a heritage of the Lord; the fruit of the womb is a reward." (127:3) When the Psalmist describes a person living in complete happiness, he promises, "Your wife shall be like a fruitful vine . . . your [children] like olive saplings around your table." (128:3) In the Book of Proverbs we are reminded, "Children's children are the crown of old men. . ." (17:6) At numerous points and in various ways, rabbinic literature tells us that the Jewish people received the Torah only for the purpose of giving it to their children. One midrash tells that,

when God offered the Torah to the Jewish people at Mount Sinai, God demanded that they produce guarantors—witnesses who would guarantee that they would take it seriously. The people offered Abraham, Isaac, and Jacob. God said, not good enough. They offered King David, but God did not accept him either. Finally, the Jewish people offered as guarantors their children and the generations of children who came after them. God accepted, saying, "Your children are good guarantors. For their sake will I give you the Torah."

The Talmud teaches that "the world is held in place by the breath of little children studying Torah." And in the Book of Isaiah we read: "All your children shall be taught of the Lord, and great shall be the peace of your children." (54:13)

Parents who have strong relationships with their children are considered blessed. The *Gemara* conveys this idea in a beautiful story told by Rabbi Isaac to Rabbi Nachman: "To what may your request for a blessing be compared? To a man who was traveling through the desert. He was hungry, tired, and thirsty when he came upon a tree, the fruits of which were sweet, its shade pleasant, and a stream of water flowing beneath it. He ate of its fruits, drank of the water, and rested under its shade. When he was about to continue his journey, he said: 'Tree, O tree, with what shall I bless you? Shall I say to you, may your fruits be sweet? They are already sweet. That your shade be pleasant? It .is already pleasant. That a stream of water flow beneath you? A stream of water already flows beneath you. Therefore I say, May it be God's will that all the shoots taken from you be like you.' So it is with you. With what shall I bless you? With the knowledge of Torah? With riches? You already have knowledge of the Torah and riches. So I say, 'May it be God's will that your offspring be like you.' "

Having children is a mitzvah, but it is only the beginning. Child rearing entails responsibilities. The rabbis taught, for example, that a father has specific obligations to his son: to arrange to circumcise him; if he is the firstborn to his mother—to provide for the ceremony of *pidyon haben;* to teach him Torah; to find a wife for him; and to teach him a craft. Rabbi Judah said, "He who does not teach his son a craft teaches him to be a robber." (Talmud) All of these obligations of a father to a son have an underlying purpose—to save life. Torah assures spiritual life; trade assures one's physical life and allows one to earn self-esteem; marriage saves one from a life of promiscuity and unhappiness. Some say a father must also teach his son to swim. At least one scholar suggests that Jews were active in commerce and often traveled in merchant ships around the Mediterranean. At times, they were attacked by pirates and hurled into the sea. Thus, knowing how to swim could certainly have helped save their lives.

Both parents have responsibility for shaping the character of their children. In the *Ve'ahavta*, we say, "You shall teach them diligently to your children." (Deut. 6:7) The same ideas are repeated throughout the Torah. For instance, we read, "Make them known to your children and your children's children: the day you stood before the Lord your God . . . when the Lord said to me, 'Gather the people to Me that I may let them hear My words, in order that they may learn to revere me as long as they live on earth, and may so teach their children.' " (Deut. 4:9–10)

The rabbinic authors of the Talmud described religious rituals in terms of parents teaching children, so as to involve the young ones. The custom of having a seder on Pesach derives from the commandment, "You shall tell your [child] in that day, saying: 'It is because of that which the Lord did for me when I came forth out of Egypt.' " (Exod. 13:8) The seder is described almost entirely in terms of parents helping their children understand and encouraging them to rejoice.

Children are encouraged to blow the shofar and may even be taught to blow the shofar on Shabbat and weekday holidays. Children should be taught to observe the fast of Yom Kippur. Of course, if their health demands it, they may eat on Yom Kippur, for one should not afflict children on the Day of Atonement by making them fast or denying them food. But one should prepare them for their adult responsibilities. "One trains them a year or two before in order that they may become used to religious observance." (Talmud)

Parents have responsibility for the intellectual and moral growth of their children, to make sure that their children learn Torah. Reform Judaism teaches that parents also are required to see that their children receive a quality secular education. There is evidence that in ancient days fathers took it upon themselves to teach their sons, while private teachers educated their daughters. The Talmud, and later Jewish commentaries, devoted attention to what a proper curriculum should include, specifying Scripture, *Mishnah,* and *Gemara.*

Jewish tradition sets standards for respectable behavior. We read in the Book of Proverbs: "A foolish son is vexation to his father, and bitterness to her that bore him" (17:25); "A wise son makes a glad father; but a foolish son is the grief of his mother." (10:1) The Haggadah identifies four different sons according to their character traits, a recognition that people have the capacity to be simple or foolish, wise or wicked—and that parents have differing responsibilities to different types of children.

Jewish sources also recognize the difficulties parents often encounter in disciplining their children. Here are some examples: "A bad son in a man's house is worse than . . . [a] war." The Torah and the Talmud teach that a stubborn and rebellious son, one who curses his parents, strikes them (Exod. 21:15), or one who is a glutton or a drunkard is subject to severe punishment. The Torah describes how the parents of such a son had a communal obligation to bring him to the city elders for discipline. On the other hand, parents are advised to forgive a stubborn and rebellious child. Parents, therefore, have the responsibility both to teach and to discipline their children.

Does Judaism sanction physical punishment of children? Proverbs 23:13 says: "Do not withhold discipline from your child; if you beat him

with a rod he will not die." And elsewhere it states, "He that spares the rod hates his son; but he that loves him chastens him at times." (Prov. 13:24) A midrash teaches: "If one refrains from punishing a child, he will end up by becoming utterly depraved." Once children have grown up, says the Talmud, parents can no longer discipline them or exert the same kind of influence.

The rabbis were also aware that it is possible for parents to be too severe in disciplining their children: "Do not terrorize your household." The ideal form of discipline involves being both firm and loving. Thus, teaches the Talmud, the right course is to "push away with the left hand and draw them near with the right hand."

Today we take a dim view of corporal punishment of children, knowing how easily it can lead to life-threatening child abuse. The rabbis did not encourage violence in the home; they wanted only to emphasize that love alone, without discipline, could not shape children into responsible adults.

WHAT DID RABBI COHEN DECIDE?

The issue in Rebecca's case was not that her parents acted without reason or care. While it seemed to Rebecca that they were dismissing her interests, they were in fact demonstrating their love for her by ensuring that she receive a good Jewish education, as required by our tradition. Their concern for her character development grows from an attitude that stresses a parent's obligation to meet the totality of a child's needs—physical, intellectual, and spiritual.

Could Rebecca's parents have acted more gently? Rabbi Cohen said, "Yes, they could have." Could they have tried to reason with her instead of just forcing her to go along with their wishes? Again, Rabbi Cohen said yes. Was it possible that Rebecca could miss a day of religious school to participate in the championship game? Rebecca was really surprised when he said yes a third time. "But . . ."—and he said this *but* with a lot of emphasis—he wanted Rebecca to understand that her parents behaved as they did not because they didn't love her but precisely because they loved her so much and were concerned about her long-term happiness and well-being. Still, it seemed all right to him if she missed a day to pursue an interest that was of utmost importance to her. Why not just do a little makeup work? In fact, Rabbi Cohen said he would be willing to call her parents and tell them that himself.

Rebecca felt better after her session with Rabbi Cohen. Her parents did care about her after all.

HAVE YOU EVER FELT LIKE REBECCA?

Share a time in your life when you were furious with your parents, when you felt that a decision they made was unfair. Are you still angry? Does their decision now make more sense? Why?

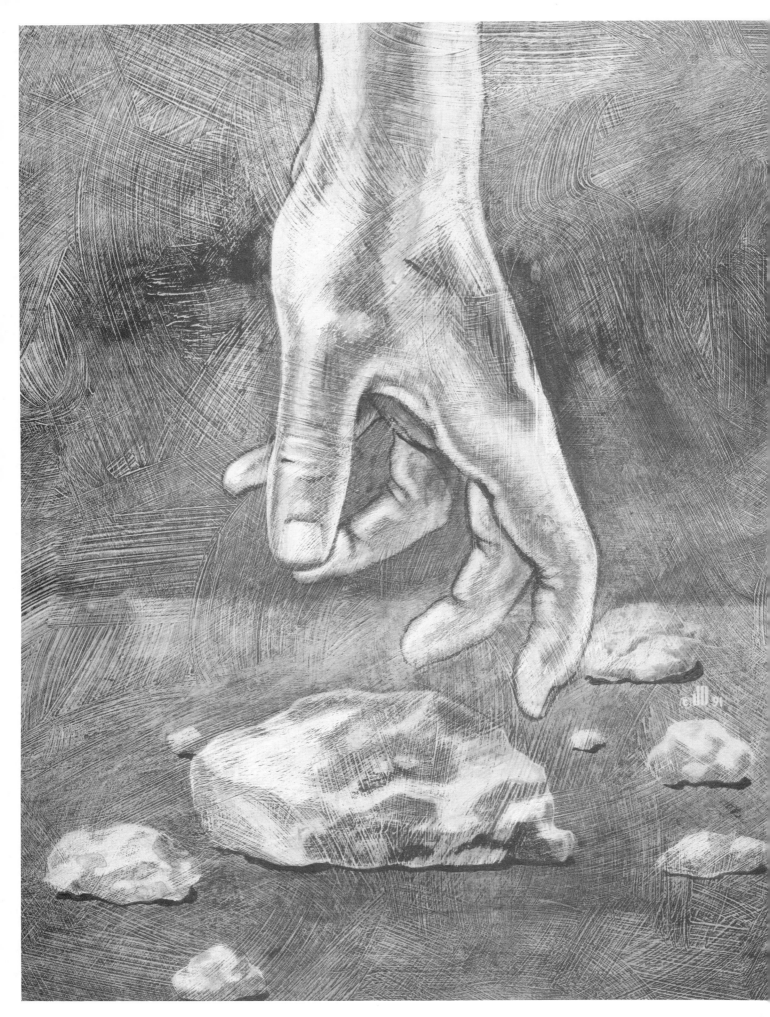

CHAPTER
10

CAPITAL PUNISHMENT:
Does the State Have the Right to Take a Life?

Emily and Janice had just returned home from religious school. They were still talking about their homework assignment for Mr. Berman's Jewish values class: prepare a Jewish perspective on one important news item. They turned on the TV that night and heard varied reactions to the execution of a convicted murderer. Foes of capital punishment demonstrated in several states. People in favor of the death penalty celebrated the execution; some even waved barbecue skewers gleefully.

"What a disgusting display," said Emily.

"I can't believe people would actually celebrate somebody else's death," agreed Janice.

"I think we should write our paper on capital punishment," said Emily. "It should be a snap. I am sure that Judaism rejects it!"

Janice frowned. "Don't be so sure. This could be really complicated."

If you had to decide right now, would you guess that Jewish law supported or opposed capital punishment? Note your answer for later reference.

The two friends studied Jewish positions on the death penalty. Here is what they found.

IN THE BIBLE

Emily and Janice began with the Torah and were surprised to discover that it prescribes capital punishment for a wide range of criminal and religious offenses: murder (Num. 35:16), idolatry (Lev. 20:2), adultery (Deut. 22:22), being a stubborn and rebellious son (Deut. 21:18–21), violation of Shabbat (Num. 15:32–36), blasphemy (Lev. 24:15–16), divination or wizardry (Lev. 20:27), and a number of acts that we might regard as being relatively minor or insignificant today.

The Torah, however, restricts the practical application of capital punishment. A person cannot be put to death unless at least two (or in some cases three) eyewitnesses testify against the accused. Each witness must be so certain of his testimony that he would be willing to carry out the execution personally.

IN THE TALMUD

The rabbis of the Talmud define a number of transgressions as deserving of death. These include adultery, idolatry, illicit sex, violating the

Sabbath, witchcraft, and for a rebellious son. They cite four means of execution, beginning with the most severe: stoning, burning, slaying by the sword, and strangulation. The rabbis were meticulous in linking each crime with its corresponding punishment.

The Talmud specifies that capital cases had to be heard by a court of twenty-three judges, and in some cases, seventy-one judges. The rabbis held judges in capital trials to a high standard: "Anyone fit to try capital cases could also try monetary cases, but a person fit to try a monetary case may still be unfit to try a capital case." Rabbi Judah says that a person disposed to be cruel should be excluded from sitting in judgment in such cases. Not only should a person's own record be pure and righteous, but it is required that even his ancestry be free of blemish before he can sit on such a court. A person cannot serve as both a judge and a witness in the same trial. If a person has witnessed a crime, it is incumbent upon him to serve as a witness before the court, and therefore he is not eligible to serve as a judge in that case. The rabbis barred certain people, such as relatives of the accused, from serving as witnesses in capital cases. So seriously did the rabbis take the proceedings of a capital trial that they disqualified whole classes of people, including gamblers and usurers, who were considered to be engaged in work that made them unfit for serious matters or insensitive to the distinctions between strict truth and falsehood.

In order to qualify as a witness, a person had to answer a series of questions, such as: Did you know [name of accused]? Did he kill a heathen? Did he kill an Israelite? Did you warn him? Did he accept your warning by saying something like "I know that I am warned not to do this"? Did he admit his liability to death [by answering something like "Even though I know I shall be punished by such and such a manner, yet I want to go ahead and commit this crime!"]?

Capital cases were tried only during the day. The judges sat on three rising semicircular tiers as in an amphitheater so that they could see one another. Two judges' clerks stood before them, one to the right and the other to the left, recording the arguments of those who would acquit and those who would condemn. Two such clerks were necessary as a precaution against any mistake. Rabbi Judah has said that there were three such clerks: one to record arguments for acquittal, a second to record arguments for conviction, and a third to record arguments for both acquittal and conviction. Witnesses stood in front of these tiers of judges.

Witnesses were asked to establish the day and year of the crime and explain the circumstances surrounding it. Then the court began to "fill the witness with fear" in order to ensure that his testimony was not based on conjecture, i.e., from circumstantial evidence, hearsay, simple rumor, or the observations of another witness.

The judge warned the witness that he would be subjected to rigorous and relentless cross-examination and held personally responsible should the accused be falsely condemned. Bearing false witness in a capital case was itself a crime punishable by death.

The rabbis disallowed circumstantial evidence. To qualify as a witness in a capital case, a person had to have seen the crime being committed. Rabbi Simeon ben Shatach describes an incident in which he was personally involved:

> I saw a man chasing another man into a ruin;
> I ran after him and saw a sword in his hand dripping with the other's blood, and the murdered man in his death agony. . . .

Still his testimony was inadmissible because he did not see the actual crime. Rabbi Simeon, however, was convinced that the criminal would pay for his crime, for "He who knows one's thoughts [will] exact vengeance from him who slew his fellow."

Beyond seeing the crime, an eligible witness in a capital case had to have forewarned the perpetrator of the consequences of the illegal act and that the contemplated crime was punishable by death. According to Rabbi Judah, the warning even had to specify the execution method. Furthermore, two or three witnesses had to be found who had gone through the above procedure of warning the accused, a very unlikely prospect. If such witnesses could be found, the court could convict the accused only if guilt could be proved beyond doubt. According to the Talmud, "A doubt in capital charges should always be for the benefit of the accused."

When the court voted, acquittal required a majority of one, condemnation a majority of two. The verdict could be reversed in favor of acquittal if errors were revealed, but not in favor of condemnation. Also, in reaching the verdict, a judge could argue in favor of the accused but not against him. One who had argued initially for condemnation might subsequently argue for acquittal, but one who had argued for acquittal could not later argue for condemnation. If a judge who argued in favor of the defendant died, the court registered a posthumous vote for acquittal.

Even after a guilty verdict, provisions were made to stay the execution. A person was stationed at the door of the court holding a flag, while a horseman stood at the ready within sight of the signalman. If one of the judges said he had something further to state in favor of the condemned, the signaler waved his flag, sending the horseman to postpone the execution. Indeed, even if the condemned said he had a further plea, the court was obliged to reconvene.

Once a sentence was pronounced, a herald was dispatched to stand in front of the condemned man and cry out: "So and so, son of so and so, is going forth to be stoned because he committed such and such offense, and so and so are his witnesses. If anyone has anything to say in his favor, let him come forward and state it." If someone offered to make a statement in favor of the condemned man, a retrial followed. If a person was pronounced innocent and someone came forward and said, "I have something to state against him," however, the defendant was not retried.

Thus, the rabbis set great obstacles in the path of capital punishment, both before and after the trial. Without rejecting the death penalty in principle, the rabbis made its implementation nearly impossible, reflecting their profound discomfort with capital punishment.

A Sanhedrin that executed a suspect once in seven years was branded a destructive tribunal. Rabbi Eleazer ben Azariah says it was to be called a destructive tribunal if it executed a suspect once in seventy years. Rabbi Tarfon and Rabbi Akiba said that, if they were members of a Sanhedrin, nobody would ever be put to death. In fact, there is an explicit statement that a bet din (law court) was considered a "murdering" bet din if it ever inflicted the death penalty.

In the same Gemara, however, Rabbi Simeon ben Gamaliel took the opposite position, saying if they never condemned anyone to death, they might also be considered guilty of promoting violence and bloodshed: "In that case, they would multiply the shedders of blood in Israel."

According to one source, capital punishment was abolished forty years before the fall of Jerusalem. The rabbis decided that, rather than apply the four methods of death penalty themselves, they would rely on divine justice. The guilty would be held accountable to God because taking a person's life, the ultimate retribution, should not be entrusted to fallible humans. This does not mean that the rabbis did not believe in punishing the guilty. They had no compunction about decreeing corporal punishment—punishment by physical suffering. In some cases, they imprisoned offenders who could not be punished by death if they were convinced of their guilt. It was not harsh sentences for the guilty that they feared, but the imposition of the death penalty.

When the Jewish state was reestablished in 1948, application of the death penalty was virtually abolished, even though the law still permitted it. When Israel's penal laws were revised in 1954, the death penalty was legally eliminated, except in the case of individuals guilty of participating in the crime of genocide or for acts of treason during warfare. Only one person has been executed in Israel's history: Adolf Eichmann, the architect of the Nazi destruction of European Jewry.

Significantly, when the very first trial for murder was held after the establishment of the State of Israel, many Jewish leaders sent cables to the Minister of Justice expressing their opposition to the sentence of death.

And why all this objection to capital punishment? The rabbis understood that a person wrongfully flogged for robbing would heal. A person improperly imprisoned for crimes of violence could be freed. But someone unjustly killed for a crime he or she did not commit could never be called back before the bar of justice and have the mistake corrected. The court and the entire society it represented would be held responsible for a terrible wrong.

The Talmud includes a chilling account of just such a miscarriage of justice. Rabbi Judah ben Tabbai admitted that he once sentenced a man to death on the basis of false testimony. The condemned man was the son of Rabbi Judah's own colleague, Simeon ben Shatach. Later the witnesses admitted that they had lied—committed perjury. The condemned man was told he could be spared, but he refused to take advantage of the offer, fearing it would look as if his father, head of the Sanhedrin, had abused his office. He went to his death, though innocent.

This incident, involving one of the members of their own circle, must have made a strong impression on the rabbis who had to decide cases, and who wrote the laws. Perhaps this tragic event mobilized the rabbis to make the imposition of the death penalty virtually impossible. The laws of capital punishment remained on the books, but their enactment was made progressively so difficult as to render them null and void in practice.

YOUR ANSWER

Now that you have reviewed some important sources concerning the Jewish stance on capital punishment, reread your answer to the question posed at the beginning of this chapter: "Does Jewish law support or oppose capital punishment?"

Do you still agree with your original answer? If not, how would you revise it? Write a one-page report that you think Emily and Janice should have submitted to Mr. Berman.

JUDAISM AND CAPITAL PUNISHMENT

by Emily and Janice

We watched the evening news report on the execution of a murderer and decided to find out what Judaism had to say about capital punishment.

While we were surprised by the large number of crimes punishable by death in the Bible, we discovered on closer reading that capital punishment has been virtually nonexistent in Judaism for close to two thousand years. While the laws of the Torah still exist, subsequent generations imposed so many restrictions upon enforcement of capital crimes that the death penalty could not be carried out.

Even in the State of Israel, where the government could have enacted death penalty legislation, the only execution in the nation's history has been that of a brutal Nazi leader, guilty of ordering the genocide of millions of innocent Jewish men, women, and children.

Except in the rarest of cases, Judaism opposes capital punishment, and any taking of human life.

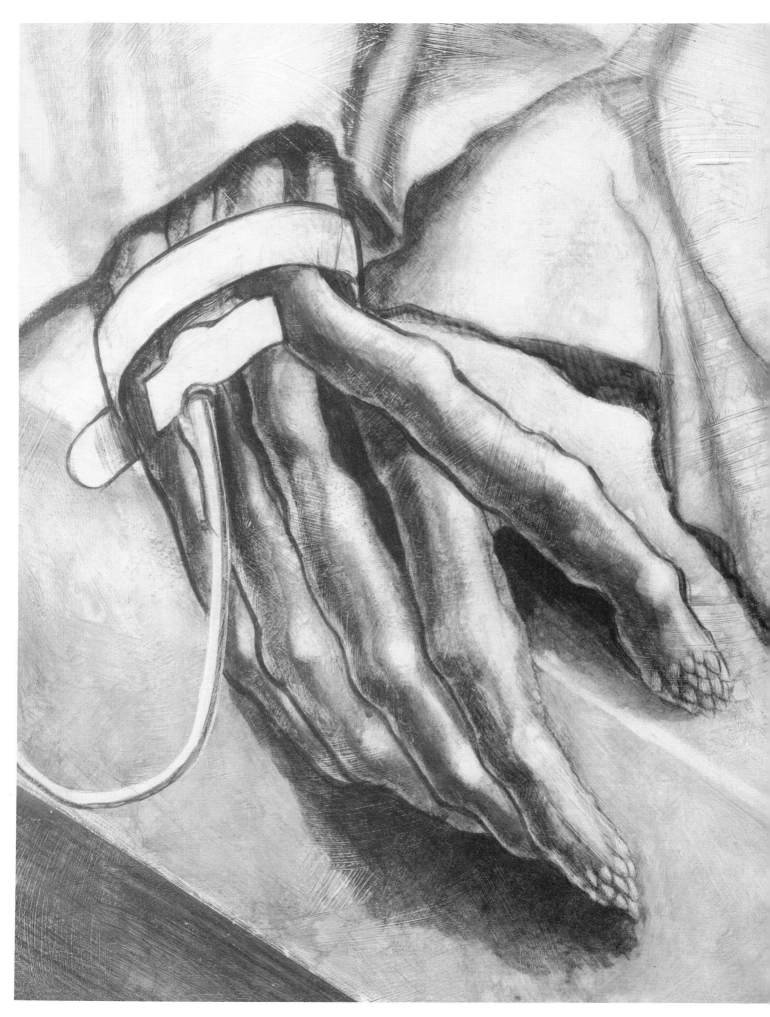

CHAPTER

11

EUTHANASIA:
Should We Help People to Die?

On April 15, 1974, a young woman named Karen Quinlan lapsed into a coma in a New Jersey hospital. But at the time no one could have foreseen that the tragedy would become known in international religious, medical, and legal circles as a test case to determine the limits of doctors in making life-and-death decisions.

Tens of thousands of people lapse into comas every year. Half of them die within forty-eight hours. Of those who survive longer, 81 percent attain at least some recovery after a year, but as in the case of Karen Quinlan, 3 percent slip into a persistent vegetative state. Although the doctors agreed that there was no hope of recovery, they attached her to a respirator to prolong her life.

Karen Quinlan would probably have remained a tragic but anonymous statistic had it not been for the fact that her parents, as a merciful act, instructed her doctors to disconnect the respirator and to allow her to die in peace. The doctors refused, asserting that it was their duty to preserve life no matter what the prognosis and that to follow the parents' wishes would be an act of murder. Karen's parents disagreed

and sued the hospital for the right to remove this artificial life-maintenance system.

The ensuing court case attracted worldwide media attention. Doctors, religious leaders, families of coma patients, and the public debated the case for months. Finally, the court reached a decision.

What would Judaism say? Does a person have the right to die? Does anyone have the right to "pull the plug"?

ACTIVE EUTHANASIA

The word "euthanasia" comes from two Greek words, *eu* (pleasant) and *thanatos* (death), and refers to any act in which one person "helps" another to die, usually in the face of an incurable illness or debilitating pain. For this reason, euthanasia is also referred to as "mercy killing."

The value of *pikuach nefesh*, "saving a life," is paramount in Judaism. Life is sacred, and preserving life takes precedence over virtually every other mitzvah. Therefore, it should come as no surprise that Jewish law prohibits *active* euthanasia, considering it tantamount to murder.

A single example will help to explain what we mean by active euthanasia. Several years ago, the national press reported about an elderly man whose wife was suffering from terminal cancer and experiencing excruciating pain despite all medication. During one of her husband's visits to her hospital room, the woman begged her husband to help release her from her agony. She felt degraded by her illness and suffered great pain.

At first her husband refused. But, after several days of hearing her emotional pleas, he purchased a gun, returned to the hospital, tenderly kissed his wife, then shot and killed her. The husband claimed that his actions were merciful and far more humane than extended medical treatment. The court found the husband guilty of murder but, because of his advanced age, did not sentence him to prison.

Jewish law would have concurred in the court's verdict. The legal precedents are quite clear. Judaism views the soul as a guest in the body. Since God originally gave the soul, no human being can take it back. Therefore murder, active euthanasia, suicide, or any act that hastens death is forbidden.

IN THE BIBLE

Only God Can Take a Life

Each book of the Torah contains at least one prohibition against murder, in addition to the sixth commandment of the Ten Commandments, "You shall not murder." A passage from the Book of Deuteronomy makes explicit the biblical view that no human being has the right to "play God":

> See now that I, even I, am He, and there is no God with Me; I [alone] kill, and I make alive. . . .   (32:39)

In the Book of Job, we see a concrete instance of a refusal to challenge the prerogative belonging only to God. Job suffers terrible afflictions, losing his wealth and children. His skin is covered with boils and bleeding sores. His wife urges Job to curse God and die. But Job responds:

> What? Shall we receive good at the hand of God, and shall we not receive evil? For all this did not Job sin with his lips.   (2:10)

A Case of Active Euthanasia

One case of active euthanasia recorded in the Bible is that of King Saul. Scripture relates:

> Now the Philistines fought against Israel, and the men of Israel fled from before the Philistines, and fell down slain in Mount Gilboa. And the Philistines followed hard upon Saul. . . . And the battle went sore against Saul, and the archers overtook him; and he was in great anguish by reason of the archers. Then said Saul to his armor-bearer: "Draw your sword, and thrust me through, lest [the enemy] come and thrust me through . . ." But his armor-bearer would not; for he was sore afraid. Therefore Saul took his sword, and fell upon it. . . . So Saul died. . . .   (I Samuel 31:1–6)

From this passage it appears that Saul committed suicide. However, in the next passage, it becomes clear that Saul's attempt at suicide failed, for he asks an Amalekite to slay him to help him die more quickly, in effect to engage in active euthanasia.

> And [Saul] said unto me, "Stand . . . beside me, and slay me. . . ." So I stood beside him, and slew him . . . [helped him to die].
>   (II Samuel 1:9–10)

At least three great medieval rabbinic commentators, Rabbi David Kimchi, Rabbi Levi ben Gershom, and Rashi consider this a case of active euthanasia. Apparently, so did King David, who immediately ordered the Amalekite condemned and executed for murder!

IN THE RABBINIC PERIOD

In the rabbinic period the same attitude displayed by Job was shown by Rabbi Chanina ben Teradion. As he was being burned by the Romans for teaching Torah, in violation of their edict, and as the flames enveloped him, his students called out, "Open your mouth so that the fire can enter you [and put an end to your agony]." He replied, "Let Him [God] who gave me [my soul] take it away, but no one should injure himself [i.e., hasten his own death]." (Talmud)

The Talmud declares that a dying individual is a living person and therefore forbids any act that conceivably could hasten death: "A dying person is considered as a living person in all respects. . . ."

This view was shared by Maimonides and Joseph Karo, two of Judaism's greatest legal authorities.

According to Jewish law, one may not close the eyes of a dying person to hasten death. Rabbi Meir used to cite an example of a flickering light: "As soon as a person touches it, it goes out. So, too, whoever closed the eyes of the dying is as if he has taken his soul." (Talmud) The prohibitions against hastening death are also enumerated in later rabbinic sources. The *Tur*, a Jewish legal code written by Jacob ben Asher, lists a series of prohibitions with regard to the dying under the general guideline that "any act performed in relation to death should not be carried out until the soul has departed." Joseph Karo, in his *Code of Jewish Law*, devotes an entire chapter to the laws of the dying person, listing various acts that are prohibited, "lest they hasten the patient's death."

In summary, then, Jewish law makes no provision for active euthanasia, even in cases when the patient endures great suffering.

PASSIVE EUTHANASIA

In Karen Quinlan's case, the issue was whether or not a doctor had the right to withhold "he-roic" mechanical treatment whose sole purpose was to artificially prolong a life that they believed could not have persisted unaided. Stated differently, what are the limits upon the freedom of action of a physician with regard to a dying patient? By "dying patient" we mean a person capable of being healed. If, for example, a person has a heart attack and can be treated, or if a person has been rescued from drowning and can be saved with resuscitation, such a dying patient must be afforded every medical resource. The Talmud clearly indicates that one may risk experimental or otherwise forbidden remedies if the dying patient has a chance of being cured by them. Any or all medicine and drugs must be used to help an individual recover. Even the laws of Shabbat may be broken to save a life.

But what about Karen Quinlan? What about patients for whom doctors have no hope?

On this question Jewish law is clear. The doctor is not obligated to force a patient to live a few more days or hours. This stance is derived from a famous incident described in the Talmud. The great Rabbi Judah the Prince, who compiled the *Mishnah*, was dying and in great suffering. His devoted students tried to save his life by praying outside of his house around the clock. He hovered between life and death, but in great distress. Rabbi Judah's servant could not stand to see him suffer so. She knew that, if she could stop his students from praying, Rabbi Judah's "soul could leave his body" and he would die in peace. She therefore climbed to the roof of the house and threw down an earthen jar. Distracted by the noise, the students stopped praying for an instant. At that moment Rabbi Judah died. In the Talmud, the servant is praised by the rabbis for her intervention.

The Spanish scholar Nissim Gerondi says that, while it is our duty to pray for a sick person's recovery, there are also times when we should pray for God's mercy in bringing death. So, too, a book entitled *Sefer Chasidim* states: "If a man is dying, we do not pray too hard that his soul will return and that he will revive from the coma. He can, at best, live only a few days and in those days will endure great suffering. So 'there is a time to die.' "

In other words, according to the spirit of Jewish tradition, just as a person has a right to live, so there come times when a person has a right to die. Thus, there is no duty incumbent upon the physician to force a terminal patient to live a little longer. But what, under these circumstances, is a physician actually permitted to do?

We have already seen that the doctor may do nothing active to hasten death. However, Rabbi Judah ben Samuel the Pious, also in *Sefer Chasidim*, states that one has a right to stop acts that would hinder the soul's departure. If someone outside is chopping wood, for example, and that rhythmic sound distracts the dying patient and prevents the soul from departing, you may stop the wood chopping so that the patient may relax and die in peace. Or, if there is salt on a patient's tongue and the tartness of the salt focuses the patient's mind and keeps him or her from relaxing into death, you may wipe the salt from the tongue and thus allow the patient to die.

Moses Isserles in the *Shulchan Aruch* sums up what is permitted and what is not permitted by saying that such things are permitted that "do not involve action at all, but merely remove that which hinders death." Rabbi Solomon Eiger goes even further in saying that "it is forbidden to hinder the departure of the soul by the use of medicines."

In summary, all rabbinic authorities agree that under no circumstances is the *hastening* of death (euthanasia) permitted. However, it is not necessary to utilize medical technology to sustain the life of a person in a vegetative state diagnosed as incapable of recovery.

The question, however, remains as to when independent life ceases. According to *halachah*, lack of respiratory activity and heartbeat constitutes death. In the responsum of the Chatam Sofer, lack of respiration alone was considered conclusive if "the individual lay as quietly as a stone." According to some halachic authorities, death has occurred when there is no movement for at least fifteen minutes. Others say one hour after cessation of respiration and heartbeat. Jacob Levy, an Israeli doctor, claims that lack of blood flow and respiratory activity determine death.

Because of recent advances in science, the question of when independent life ceases has become a matter of dispute. Medical science has introduced a new concept in determining when someone has died: brain death. An ad hoc committee at Harvard Medical School set the definition of brain death as having several criteria: (1) lack of response to external stimuli; (2) absence of movement and breathing as observed by physicians over a period of at least one hour; (3) absence of elicitable reflexes; and a fourth criterion to confirm the other three, a flat or isolectric electroencephalogram.

Modern Orthodox halachists have responded to this Harvard definition in various ways. Rabbi Moshe Feinstein felt that the Harvard definition could be accepted if the respirator was shut off briefly to see if there was independent breathing. Rabbi Moshe Tendler accepts Harvard's criteria, whereas Rabbis David Bleich and Jacob Levy reject it.

YOUR ANSWER

Now that we have surveyed some Jewish legal sources, it's time for you to answer the question: "According to Jewish teachings, should Karen Quinlan's doctors have disconnected her respirator?"

Write your answer and defend it.

THE JEWISH ANSWER

Given the circumstances of the Karen Quinlan case, *halachah* would allow the doctors to disconnect the respirator. Without question, Jewish law would permit the doctors to withhold any additional treatment, whether mechanical support, medication, or other extraordinary measures. Since the machine was already attached, though, removing it could have been interpreted as constituting an act that hastened death.

After great and careful consideration, however, a ruling was issued that placed "pulling the plug" in the same category as Rabbi Judah ben Samuel's removing the salt on the tongue of a dying person. In the context of such an interpretation, terminating treatment would be permitted.

THE JUDGES' ANSWER

In 1976 the New Jersey Supreme Court ruled that Karen Quinlan could be removed from the respirator and thus reached the conclusion compatible with Jewish law. In January 1985 the court ruled that all life-sustaining medical treatment, including feeding tubes, can be withheld or withdrawn from patients, provided that is what the patient wants or would want.

LIVING WILLS

In part because of the Karen Quinlan case, many individuals have begun to create "living wills," legal documents that allow victims of a terminal illness from which there is no hope of recovery to instruct a physician not to prolong life by artificial means. Copies of this document may be given to a physician, rabbi, lawyer, and to as many family members and/or friends as you desire. To sign such a document you must be eighteen years or older and of sound mind. If at any time you wish to revoke the document, you are free to do so.

The living will does not give anyone permission to end the life of another through "mercy killing." It is simply a document stating that one does not want to have life prolonged artificially after a physician decides there is no hope of recovery.

Not every state accepts a living will as legally binding. You must check with an attorney to ascertain if your state will accept this kind of will.

EPILOGUE

Karen Quinlan's parents did have the respirator disconnected. But, contrary to every medical expectation, she remained alive and in a coma another ten years, totally unaware of the agonizing questions her case forced the nation to confront.

CHAPTER

12

INTERMARRIAGE:
Why Does It So Upset Jews?

Most of the stories in this book focus on individuals and their dilemmas. This chapter is different. It concerns the fate of the entire Jewish people, as well as each of us privately.

YOUR PERSONAL DECISION

If current statistics are correct, 25 to 40 percent of Jews who marry choose a spouse who is not Jewish by birth or who has not converted to Judaism. Before we talk about the issue of intermarriage, write out your answers to two questions:

1. Why do you think Jews talk so much about this issue?
2. Do you think religion ought to be a major factor in determining whom you date or marry?

INTERMARRIAGE IN JEWISH HISTORY

From the earliest period of Jewish history, the question of intermarriage has been a highly charged issue for some Jewish families, but not

so for others. Abraham, for example, worried about it in Genesis 24, when he made his servant Eliezer swear that, in finding a wife for Isaac, "you will not take a wife for my son from the daughters of the Canaanites." It appears to have kept Rebekah up nights in Genesis 27:46, when she exclaimed: "If Jacob takes a wife of the daughters of Heth . . . what good shall my life do me?" In Genesis 28:1, Isaac commanded Jacob, "You shall *not* take a wife of the daughters of Canaan." In contrast, Jacob kept calm when, in Genesis 34, he accepted the possibility that his daughter, Dinah, might marry a non-Jew named Shechem. Jacob's sons, however, attacked Shechem's camp and slaughtered all his men in retaliation for Shechem's rape of their sister. As we are all reminded every Purim, Esther's marriage to Ahasuerus caused Mordecai no concern. Recall also that when Aaron and Miriam mock their brother, Moses, for marrying a Cushite woman, they are severely chastised by God. (Num. 12)

INTERMARRIAGE IN MODERN TIMES

Intermarriage concerns us today because it is perceived as a threat to Jewish survival. During the Nazi Holocaust, one-third of the world's Jewish population was annihilated. Today our low birth rate and assimilation keep our numbers at below replacement levels. And intermarriage, a manifestation of assimilation, is part of the price the North American Jewish community pays for the privilege of living in an open, egalitarian society.

The Jewish community's objection to intermarriage is not the result of believing ourselves to be superior to other people. Rather, the objection to intermarriage has deep roots in our religious tradition. The Central Conference of American Rabbis—the international body of Reform rabbis—reflects this view in a resolution passed in 1909 and reaffirmed in 1947:

> The CCAR declares that mixed marriages are contrary to the tradition of the Jewish religion and should, therefore, be discouraged by the American rabbinate.

The issue was raised again at the CCAR's annual convention in Atlanta, Georgia, in 1973. After a heated debate, the Conference reasserted and sustained its historic position that rabbis should not officiate at mixed marriages:

> The Central Conference of American Rabbis, recalling its stand adopted in 1909 "that mixed marriage is contrary to the Jewish tradition and should be discouraged," now declares its opposition to participation by its members in any ceremony which solemnizes a mixed marriage.

The CCAR recognizes that historically its members have held and continue to hold divergent interpretations of Jewish tradition. In order to keep open every channel to Judaism for those who have already entered into mixed marriage, the CCAR calls upon its members:

1. To assist fully in educating as Jews children of such mixed marriages.
2. To provide the opportunity for conversion of the non-Jewish spouse.
3. To encourage a creative and consistent cultivation of involvement in the Jewish community and the synagogue.

RABBINIC ROOTS OF THE MODERN POSITION

Rabbinical prohibitions against intermarriage are far broader than those specified in the Torah. The Bible prohibits marriage only with *certain* peoples: "You shall not intermarry with them [the Hittites, the Girgashites, the Amorites, the Canaanites, the Perizzites, the Hivites, and the Jebusites]: do not give your daughters to their sons or take their daughters for your sons. For they will turn your children away from Me to worship other gods, and the Lord's anger will blaze forth against you and He will promptly wipe you out." (Deut. 7:3,4)

The Bible, however, seems to permit intermarriage with people *other* than from these groups. Joseph married an Egyptian woman. (Gen. 41:45) Moses married the daughter of Jethro, a priest of Midian. (Exod. 2:16ff.) Later he took a Cushite woman as his wife as well. (Num. 12) King Solomon, according to the Bible, had one thousand wives, among them an Egyptian princess (I Kings 3:1) and Naamah, an Ammonite woman. (I Kings 14:21, 31)

Only after the destruction of the First Temple in Jerusalem was the prohibition against marrying outside the Jewish faith expanded by Ezra and Nehemiah (10:31) to include *all non-Jews*:

> Then Ezra the priest got up and said to them, "You have trespassed by bringing home foreign women, thus aggravating the guilt of Israel. So now, make confession to the Lord, God of your fathers, and do His will, and separate yourselves from the peoples of the land and from the foreign women."
>
> (Ezra 10:10–11)

Marriage restrictions in this instance may be viewed as a response to a national disaster, when the very survival of the Jewish people was at stake.

THE BOOK OF RUTH

The story of Ruth bridges the biblical and rabinic attitudes toward intermarriage. Ruth is the first convert to Judaism named in the Bible. She married her first Jewish husband, Mahlon, in the land of Moab before she embraced Judaism. After Mahlon's death, Ruth married Boaz, also a Jew, in the land of Judea. But before marrying Boaz, Ruth said to her mother-in-law Naomi: "For wherever you go, I will go; wherever you lodge, I will lodge; your people shall be my people, and your God my God." (Ruth 1:16) The rabbis interpreted this statement as an act of conversion, thus lifting the prohibition against marrying outside the faith if conversion took place. In short, marriage outside of the faith was still acceptable when Ruth married Mahlon. By the time of her second marriage, however, marriage to an unconverted non-Jew was not permitted.

Both the biblical and rabbinic rationale for opposing intermarriage seems to be that such marriages would lead to conversion out of Judaism through idolatry. (Talmud) In fact, the rabbis found the idea of intermarriage so unnerving that, at times, where it was obvious that such a marriage took place in the Torah, they reinterpreted the biblical text to convey a totally different idea. For example, the Talmud could not conceive that Judah, the great grandson of Abraham, would marry a "Canaanite." (Gen. 38:2) The rabbis, therefore, reinterpreted the verse "And Judah saw there a daughter of a certain Canaanite (*Kena'ani*)" (Gen. 38:2) to mean the daughter of "a merchant" rather than "a Canaanite," basing their interpretation on a possible alternate translation of the word *Kena'an* as "trafficker" or "merchant." (See Hosea 12:8.)

The rabbis prohibited Israelite men and women from marrying non-Jews. (Talmud) To help guard against intermarriage, they even prohibited the purchase of essential foods from heathen women, thereby reducing the chances that Jewish men might meet them. The rabbis were concerned especially with preserving Jewish group identity through the family. When there was doubt about a person's Jewishness, the rabbis took a hard line, declaring a person of doubtful Jewish status to be a non-Jew.

WHAT IF INTERMARRIAGE DID TAKE PLACE?

Whenever an intermarriage did take place, the rabbis first scrutinized the status of children. The Talmud says that, in a marriage between a Jew and a non-Jew, the child is Jewish if the mother is Jewish. This is called matrilineal descent. However, according to Reform practice, and in keeping with the Central Conference of American Rabbis' resolution of 1983 on patrilineal descent, the child of either a Jewish man or a Jewish woman will be presumed to be Jewish if he or she is raised to be Jewish, receives a Jewish education, and participates in the appropriate Jewish rites of passage, such as circumcision, bar/bat mitzvah, and confirmation.

Historically, opposition to marriages between Jews and non-Jews was upheld by the Catholic Church as well. The Council of Elvira, about 300 C.E., forbade its females to wed non-Catholics; Pope Innocent III decreed through the Fourth Lateran Council in 1215 that Jews must wear distinctive garb, thus marking and separating Jews from Christians in order to prevent intermarriage.

As contact between Jews and non-Jews increased, so did intermarriage, a phenomenon that the Jewish community regarded with distress and sorrow. Often, a family would observe *shivah*, that is, engage in actual mourning rites for a person entering such a union. To all intents and purposes, he or she was dead—cut off from the living Jewish community.

The vast majority of North American Jews no longer take such a harsh view of intermarriage. Rarely will a family respond by sitting *shivah*, except among the ultra-Orthodox. Most Jewish parents and grandparents, however, discourage their children and grandchildren from marrying a person of another religion.

WHAT ABOUT INTERDATING?

Some Jews oppose interdating because going out with someone who is not Jewish influences future marriage choices. Through dating we develop not only social skills but also spouse-selection skills. Recent studies show that people who date those of other faiths are more likely to marry outside of their faith.

WHAT SHOULD WE CONSIDER?

If a Jew considers marriage to a non-Jew, three immediate issues arise. The first is marital compatibility. Studies have shown that marriages work better when the partners come from similar social, religious, ethnic, and cultural backgrounds. Interreligious marriages have a higher rate of dissatisfaction and divorce than same-religion marriages. Some parental objections to intermarriage, therefore, come from a concern about their child's future well-being and happiness.

The second issue concerns one's personal religious identity. We have to ask how much Jewish cultural or religious life matters. If it is important, it may very well be more difficult to compromise in a marriage in which a spouse does not share our Jewishness, especially with regard to life-cycle events and holiday celebrations.

Finally, there is the question of the future of the Jewish people. It may sound unrealistic to talk about such a "big issue," when the question at hand ostensibly concerns friendship and love. But confront it we must. If the high rate of intermarriage continues, in a few generations the Jewish population may suffer a steep decline. So each one of us has to ask: How important to me is Jewish survival? How much do I care about preserving this unique and rich strand in the tapestry of human history?

If we want Jewish life to exist in the future, we have to do our part to preserve it. And that part involves not only giving to Jewish causes or attending worship services. One of the most important contributions each one of us can make will be reflected in our personal life choices, the most crucial being whom we marry and in which tradition we raise our children.

Look at the answers you wrote at the beginning of the chapter. Would you answer them differently now?

CONCLUSION

Now that you have completed this book, you have some idea of the wide range of issues addressed by Jewish law.

We hope that you will help us plan for additional volumes in this series by writing to us with questions you'd like to have answered.

Send your questions to:

What Does Judaism Say?
c/o Rabbi Daniel B. Syme
838 Fifth Avenue
New York, NY 10021

Good luck in your future studies and in your growth as a literate Jew!

AUTHORS' NOTE

This book contains sources from many volumes of Jewish legend and law. Since footnoting each source would have been a great distraction to readers, we made a conscious decision to simplify the process.

All quotes from the Hebrew Bible are specified by book, chapter, and verse and are either from the Standard Jewish Version (1955) or the New Jewish Version (1961), both published by the Jewish Publication Society.

All citations from the Talmud are designated as Talmud, and the quotations are derived primarily from the Soncino Talmud and also from the Danby *Mishnah*.

Any story or teaching from a midrashic collection is noted as Midrash.

We are grateful for your understanding.

Temple Israel

Minneapolis, Minnesota

IN MEMORY OF
IRVING GREENBERG
FROM
EDWIN & MARGERY HARRIS